THE
ENGLAND
COMPENDIUM

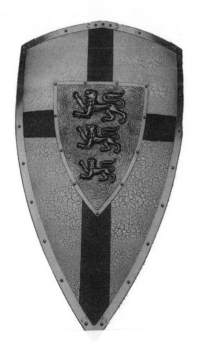

THE
ENGLAND
COMPENDIUM

THE GREATEST
ENGLAND FOOTBALL
TRIVIA BOOK EVER

CLIVE BATTY

VSP

Text © Clive Batty

Illustrations © Bob Bond Sporting Caricatures

Printed and bound in the UK by Cromwell Press

Editor: Jim Drewett
Illustrated by: Bob Bond
Cover design: David Hicks
Typeset by: Dave Jackson
Cover pic: Empics
Shield pic: www.spiral.org

Typeset by Palimpsest Book Production Limited,
Polmont, Stirlingshire

A CIP catalogue record for this book is available from the British Library

ISBN 1-905326-07-6

— INTRODUCTION —

It might bring you out in a cold sweat but, just for a minute, cast your mind back to those grey days when Graham Taylor was England manager. Possibly the most reviled England boss of all time, among the many criticisms of the man *The Sun* dubbed 'The Turnip' was the fact that he appeared to choose his teams on an almost completely random basis. The result? Journeymen pros like Earl Barrett, Geoff Thomas and Carlton Palmer got called up for England duty in a turn of events which probably surprised them as much as it did the nation's football followers.

Pick 'n' mix didn't quite work for Taylor as a selection policy – OK, let's be honest, it was a complete and utter disaster – but that's not to say it couldn't work in the right circumstances. Take this book, for instance.

The England Compendium is a potpourri of just about everything and anything related to the England football team since the Three Lions first roared into action against Scotland in 1872. So, inside these pages you'll find facts, figures, records, tables and lists galore along with numerous quotes, anecdotes and reminiscences. With entries including England's complete playing record in the World Cup and European Championships, profiles of the legends from Bobby Moore to David Beckham, all the glorious victories and the numbing penalty shoot-out defeats, and every England result to the end of 2005, you'll find plenty of serious stats to get your teeth into. But that's not all. The focus here is just as much on the bizarre and unlikely incidents that have decorated the national team's past, from the role played by spoon-bender supreme Uri Geller in England's triumph over Scotland at Euro 96 to the dog that found the World Cup trophy under a bush in south London. Along the way you'll also encounter the worst haircuts that made it into the England squad, the most outrageous goal celebrations and the bottle of beer that lost us the World Cup.

What you won't find, however, is anything approaching a rational, logical order for all but a handful of the entries. The book is, in that sense, a haphazard mishmash of only loosely connected elements – rather like, at the risk of bringing on that cold sweat again, 'The Turnip's' England team selections.

Clive Batty
London, February 2006

Authors note: All stats in the England Compendium are correct up to the end of February 2006

— ENGLAND'S OVERALL RECORD* —

	P	W	D	L	F	A
Home	366	229	85	52	894	341
Away	396	213	98	85	871	434
Neutral	71	27	20	24	97	77
TOTAL	833	469	203	161	1862	852

*As with all stats in this book, correct up to the end of February of 2006

— THE BIRTH OF ENGLAND —

The birth of the England football team owed a great deal to Charles Alcock, one of the founders of the Football Association in 1863. In 1870 Alcock conceived the idea of an international match between English and Scottish players and placed the following advertisement in *The Sportsman*, a London sports newspaper:

"From the secretary of the Football Association. A match between the leading representatives of the Scotch and English sections will be played at The Oval on Saturday, 19th February, under the auspice of the Football Association. Players duly qualified and desirous of assisting either party must communicate with Mr AF Kinnaird of 2 Pall Mall East, SW, or Mr J Kirkpatrick, Admiralty, Somerset House, WC, on behalf of the Scotch, or with Mr Charles W Alcock, Boy Court, Ludgate Hill, EC, or Mr RG Graham, 7 Finch Lane, EC, on the part of the English."

In the event, the proposed match was called off because of a thick frost covering the ground. Eventually, though, a number of games were played in London in 1870 and 1871 between the Wanderers, a team largely consisting of former public schoolboys, and a group of Scots based in the capital. However, these were unofficial internationals as the Scottish side was selected by the English FA and included a handful of 'ringers', some of whom would go on to represent England.

At the beginning of 1872 the first rugby international between England and Scotland took place in Edinburgh. Impressed by the interest aroused in the game, Alcock saw an opportunity for an equivalent match under 'Association' rules. His proposal was agreed at a meeting of the FA on 3rd October 1872 and recorded in the minutes: "In order to further the interests of the Association in

Scotland, it was decided during the current season that a team should be sent to Glasgow to represent England."

In the absence of a Scottish version of the FA, Alcock's challenge was accepted by Scotland's leading club, Queens Park. The world's first ever international match was scheduled for Monday 24th November 1872. But in the days leading up to the big kick-off the Scots changed their minds, objecting that that they couldn't afford to take a day off from their jobs. Instead, the match was moved back to the following Saturday, 30th November. Sadly, Alcock, who was due to captain the England team, had to pull out after picking up a groin strain playing for the Old Etonians the week before. He ended up turning out as one of the game's two 'umpires', and did eventually appear for England in 1875, but only won the single cap. Nonetheless, his vision and organisational flair ensured that his name would go down in the annals of England football history.

— THE FIRST EVER ENGLAND TEAM —

So, the world's first ever international football match was played between England and Scotland at the West of Scotland Cricket Ground, Partick, Glasgow on 30th November 1872.

England, wearing white shirts with a three lions crest, white knickerbockers and dark blue caps, lined up in an ultra-attacking 1-2-7 formation with the following personnel:

Robert Barker (Hertfordshire Rangers)
Ernest Greenhalgh (Notts County)
Reginald de Courtney Welch (Wanderers)
Frederick Chappell (Oxford University)
William Maynard (1st Surrey Rifles)
John Brockbank (Cambridge University)
John Clegg (Wednesday FC)
Arnold Smith (Oxford University)
Cuthbert Ottoway (Oxford University, captain)
Charles Chenery (Crystal Palace)
Charles Morice (Barnes FC)

Scotland had the advantage not only of playing at home but also of fielding all 11 players from the same club, Queen's Park. England's preparations were less than ideal, on the other hand: seven of the players had arrived the previous day and spent the night in the Royal Garrick Hotel in Glasgow, but the other four travelled up from London on the sleeper train, arriving in Scotland on the morning of the match. There is also some doubt as to whether England fielded a specialist goalkeeper, as two players, Barker and Maynard, played a half each in goal.

Nonetheless, England dominated much of the match and were, perhaps, unfortunate to be held to a 0–0 draw. "England, especially forward, astonished the spectators by some very pretty dribbling, an art curious and novel," reported *The North British Mail*. Another journal, *Bell's Life*, was equally enthusiastic: "Altogether it was one of the jolliest, one of the most spirited and most pleasant matches that have ever been played according to Association rules."

Despite the lack of goals (incredibly, the next 0–0 draw between the two countries would not be until 1970) the event was deemed a success, with £102 raised in entrance money from an appreciative crowd of 4,000.

— DON'T QUOTE ME —

"Some of the people who have been picked for England recently should have written back to the FA saying: 'There must be some mistake, I can't play'."

Former England international **Raich Carter**, 1981

"I have seen things on *Star Trek: The Next Generation* that I find easier to believe than the fact that Mike Duxbury was once an England regular."

Comedian **Nick Hancock**, 1995

"It's easy to beat Brazil, you just stop them from getting within 20 yards of your goal."

Bobby Charlton, 1970

"To find a way past Bobby Moore was like searching for the exit from Hampton Court maze."

David Miller, *The Times*, 1993

"Football is like a car. You've got five gears and the trouble with the England team is that they drive all the time in fourth or fifth."

Ruud Gullit, 1995

"I've just seen Gary Lineker shake hands with Jurgen Klinsmann – it's a wonder Klinsmann hasn't fallen down."

Ron Atkinson, during the 1990 World Cup

— THE SHIRT OFF HIS BACK —

Famous England shirts sold at auction include:

Geoff Hurst's 1966 World Cup final shirt, sold at Christie's in September 2000 for £91,750

Bobby Moore's England v Brazil 1970 shirt, sold by Pele at Christie's in March 2004 for £59,750

Bobby Moore's spare 1966 World Cup final shirt, sold at a Molineux auction in September 1999 for £44,000

Paul Gascoigne's 1990 World Cup semi-final shirt – complete with tear stains – sold at Christie's in September 2004 for £28,680

Johnny Haynes' shirt from the 1959 match between England and Brazil in Rio de Janeiro, sold by Pele at Christie's in March 2004 for £9,560

— VILLAINS LEAD THE WAY —

Here's some surprising advice for any young player with ambitions to play for England: go to Aston Villa! Yes, over the years, the Midland club have provided more England internationals than any other side in the country:

Club	No. of England internationals
Aston Villa	64
Tottenham	58
Everton	57
Arsenal*	56
Liverpool	56
Manchester United	54
Blackburn Rovers	46
Sheffield Wednesday^	41
West Bromwich Albion	41
Chelsea	40

*Including Woolwich Arsenal FC and The Arsenal FC
^ Including Wednesday and The Wednesday

On a similar theme, Tottenham players have scored more goals for England (171) than those from any other club. Manchester United (165) and Liverpool (113) are the only other clubs to top the 100 goals mark.

— 100 GREATEST SPORTING MOMENTS —

In 2002 Channel 4 asked viewers to vote for their favourite sporting moments, broadcasting the results of the poll later in the year. Unsurprisingly, England matches featured heavily with 12 entries in the top 100. Heading the list was the Three Lions' superb 5–1 win in Germany, which was only pipped for first place by rower Steve Redgrave's fifth Olympic gold medal at the 2000 Games in Sydney. The England moments voted into the Top 100 were:

2. Germany 1 England 5, 2001
3. 1966 World Cup victory
6. Diego Maradona's second goal v England, 1986 World Cup
14. Michael Owen's goal v Argentina, 1998 World Cup
25. England 4 Holland 1, Euro 96
35. Paul Gascoigne's goal v Scotland, Euro 96
41. Gordon Banks' save from Pele's header, 1970 World Cup
49. Gazza's tears, England v West Germany, 1990 World Cup
57. Scotland's Tartan Army wreck Wembley, 1977
59. Stuart Pearce's penalty and celebration v Spain, Euro 96
75. John Barnes' solo goal v Brazil, 1984
94. Colombian goalkeeper Rene Higuita's 'scorpion kick' v England, 1995

— THE HOME INTERNATIONAL CHAMPIONSHIP: THE BEGINNING —

The Home International Championship was first played in 1884, making it the world's oldest international football tournament. The competition was established at a meeting of the four home football associations (England, Ireland, Scotland and Wales) in Manchester on 6th December 1882 where it was agreed to formalise the friendly meetings between the nations into an annual tournament. The meeting also agreed uniform rules; previously, the four countries all played a slightly different version of the game with the home side's rules being used when they played each other. The first round of Home Internationals were played in the spring and winter of 1884. At the end of the six games this is how the table looked:

	P	W	D	L	F	A	Pts
Scotland	3	3	0	0	10	1	6
England	3	2	0	1	12	2	4
Wales	3	1	0	2	7	8	2
Ireland	3	0	0	3	1	19	0

— PSYCHO, THE GHOST AND SNIFFER —

If you want to play at the highest level being good at football is only part of the equation; it also helps to have a memorable nickname – as this team of England internationals demonstrates . . .

1. **David 'Safe Hands' Seaman** (75 caps, 1989–2002)
2. **Colin 'Nijinsky' Bell** (48 caps, 1968–75)
3. **Stuart 'Psycho' Pearce** (78 caps, 1987–99)
4. **Bryan 'Captain Marvel' Robson** (90 caps, 1980–91)
5. **Martin 'The Ghost' Peters** (67 caps, 1966–74)
6. **Dennis 'The Rat' Wise** (21 caps, 1991–2000)
7. **Kevin 'Mighty Mouse' Keegan** (63 caps, 1972–82)
8. **Nat 'The Lion of Vienna' Lofthouse** (33 caps, 1950–58)
9. **Gary 'Golden Balls' Lineker** (80 caps, 1984–92)
10. **Allan 'Sniffer' Clarke** (19 caps, 1970–75)
11. **Tom 'The Preston Plumber' Finney** (76 caps, 1947–58)

— ENGLAND AT THE WORLD CUP: 1950 —

Having declined to enter the three previous tournaments following a dispute with FIFA over payments to amateurs, England's first experience of the World Cup was not a happy one. Yet, before the competition began, hopes were high that a team containing the attacking talents of Stanley Matthews, Tom Finney, Jackie Milburn and Stan Mortensen could justify its position as joint favourites for the trophy along with the hosts, Brazil. Even the local press were thrilled by England's participation, with banner headlines proclaiming 'The Kings of Football Have Arrived'.

England's chances of success, though, were not helped by the location of their hotel, the Luxor, on Copacabana beach. At night, firecrackers were frequently set off outside the hotel, depriving the players of much-needed sleep. The sleeping pills provided by a local doctor were soon in popular demand, leaving those who took them feeling groggy the next morning. With no chef assigned to the squad, meanwhile, manager Walter Winterbottom did much of the cooking.

Following a routine win over Chile in which Mortenson headed England's first ever World Cup goal, the team travelled from Rio to the mining town of Belo Horizonte to play surprise qualifiers, the USA. Facing a side who had only been invited to participate in Brazil after a number of other countries withdrew, England's stars were expected to win convincingly but, after missing a host of chances and hitting the woodwork five times, they were beaten 1–0 in one of the tournament's biggest ever shocks.

News of the result was greeted with utter astonishment around the world. Indeed, many newspapers believed the score they received down the wires must have been a mistake and changed the score to 10–1. If only. England could still have qualified for the knock-out stages by beating group leaders Spain, but went down to another narrow defeat. Dumped out of the World Cup in the most humiliating way imaginable, the team returned home with some very famous reputations in tatters.

Group table

	P	W	D	L	F	A	Pts
Spain	3	3	0	0	6	1	6
England	3	1	0	2	2	2	2
Chile	3	1	0	2	5	6	2
USA	3	1	0	2	4	8	2

Date	Venue	Result
25th June 1950	Rio de Janeiro	England 2 Chile 0
29th June 1950	Belo Horizonte	England 0 USA 1
2nd July 1950	Rio de Janeiro	England 0 Spain 1

England squad: Jimmy Dickinson (Portsmouth, 3 apps), **Tom Finney** (Preston, 3 apps), **Lawrence Hughes** (Liverpool, 3 apps), **Stan Mortensen** (Blackpool, 3 apps), **Alf Ramsey** (Tottenham, 3 apps), **Bert Williams** (Wolves, 3 apps), **Billy Wright** (Wolves, 3 apps), **John Aston** (Manchester United, 2 apps), **Roy Bentley** (Chelsea, 2 apps), **Wilf Mannion** (Middlesbrough, 2 apps), **Jimmy Mullen** (Wolves, 2 apps), **Eddie Bailey** (Tottenham, 1 app), **Bill Eckersley** (Blackburn, 1 app), **Stanley Matthews** (Blackpool, 1 app), **Jackie Milburn** (Newcastle, 1 app), **Henry Cockburn** (Manchester United, 0 apps), **Ted Ditchburn** (Tottenham, 0 apps), **Bill Nicholson** (Tottenham, 0 apps), **Lawrence Scott** (Arsenal, 0 apps), **Jim Taylor** (Fulham, 0 apps), **Bill Watson** (Sunderland, 0 apps)

Goalscorers: Mannion 1, Mortensen 1

Tournament winners: Uruguay

They said it

"Walter [Winterbottom] tried to calm things down during the interval, telling us to be patient, but it had begun to feel as though we could play for a week and not score."
Roy Bentley, on England's failure to break down the American defence

"It was the biggest freak result I ever experienced throughout my playing career. I promise you that 99 times out of a hundred we would have won the match."
> **Billy Wright**, recalling England's defeat in the same match

"We were ignorant. I had no realisation of what taking part in a World Cup – especially in a foreign country – would entail, and nor had the players. The hotel was rowdy and the food was awful."
> England manager **Walter Winterbottom**

— LEGENDARY LINE-UP —

This is how England lined up for the World Cup final against West Germany at Wembley on 30th July 1966:

1
Gordon Banks

2   **5**   **6**   **3**
George Cohen   **Jack Charlton**   **Bobby Moore**   **Ray Wilson**

4
Nobby Stiles

7   **16**
Alan Ball   **Martin Peters**

9
Bobby Charlton

10   **21**
Geoff Hurst   **Roger Hunt**

As is the custom at World Cup tournaments, the players wore squad numbers that were assigned at the start of the competition. Jimmy Greaves had the number eight shirt and Manchester United winger John Connelly was number eleven, but neither player figured after the group stage.

— WALTER AND THE SELECTORS —

England's first manager, Walter Winterbottom, had substantially more limited powers than his successors and only named his side after conferring with a panel of FA bigwigs, the International Selection Committee:

"When I first started there were eight of them plus a chairman. We would all meet in the Victoria Hotel, Sheffield, because it was a central location. We would all sit down around a big table and the chairman would say, 'Now, gentlemen, it's time we picked the team. Let's have the nominations for goalkeeper' – and there would be five or six names put forward. Then we would have to whittle it down to one. That's how it was done. It often went on for hours as the selectors, some of whom had not even watched the player talked about, would argue it out. A lot of it in those days was recognition for loyalty to a club. A player might be given a cap if the selectors felt he had been a faithful servant of the club."

From *The Second Most Important Job in the Country* **by Niall Edworthy (Virgin Publishing Ltd, 1999)**

— PENALTY FLOPS —

Just three players have missed more than one penalty for England (discounting penalty shoot-outs). Most famously, David Beckham lofted a spot-kick against Turkey well over the bar in England's European Championship qualifier in Istanbul on 11th October 2003. Then, at the tournament proper against France, he saw his penalty saved by goalkeeper Fabian Barthez. The miss proved crucial, as England eventually went down to a 2–1 defeat.

The two other players to miss twice from the spot were Roger Byrne (against Brazil and Yugoslavia in 1956) and Francis Lee (against Wales and Portugal in 1969).

— ONE DAY, TWO MATCHES —

On three occasions in the late nineteenth century England played two games on the same day. Fortunately, perhaps, none of the players involved actually appeared in both games as the England selectors chose two entirely different teams for the games against Wales and Ireland, which were viewed as trial matches for the much more important fixture later in the season against Scotland. Although somewhat unusual, the policy worked well enough as England won all three 'double headers' during this period:

Date	Venue	Result
15th March 1890	Belfast	Ireland 1 England 9
15th March 1890	Wrexham	Wales 1 England 3
7th March 1891	Sunderland	England 4 Wales 1
7th March 1891	Wolverhampton	England 6 Ireland 1
5th March 1892	Wrexham	Wales 0 England 2
5th March 1892	Belfast	Ireland 0 England 2

Although not quite in the same category of fixture congestion, in June 1982 England played two matches on consecutive days against Iceland and Finland. However, no players appeared in both games, with the team that drew 1–1 in Reykjavik being largely composed of reserve players. The following day, 3rd June 1982, the full England side beat Finland 4–1 in Helsinki.

— C.B. FRY: A SPORTING PHENOMENON —

Although he only won a single cap, against Ireland in 1901, C.B. (Charles Burgess) Fry was one of the most remarkable men to represent England at football.

Possibly the greatest all-round sportsman ever, Fry played soccer for Corinthians and Southampton, appearing in the FA Cup final for the Saints in 1902. Previously, at Oxford, he won twelve Blues and captained the university at soccer, athletics and cricket in the same year – an unprecedented achievement. An outstanding cricketer, Fry played 26 Tests for England and was undefeated in a short stint as captain of the side. For Sussex, where he formed a formidable partnership with fellow England international Prince Ranjitsinhji, he averaged over 50 in first-class matches. At rugby, he played for Oxford, Blackheath and the Barbarians, and could have played for England. He held the world long-jump record for two years after leaping 23 feet 5 inches in 1892, but missed out on competing at the 1896 Olympics as he didn't know they were taking place. Fry's supreme athleticism was demonstrated by his favourite party piece, jumping backwards onto a mantelpiece from a standing position.

But Fry was much more than a sportsman. He won a scholarship to Oxford, where his friends numbered the writers Max Beerbohm and Hilaire Belloc and his nicknames included 'Charles III', 'Almighty' and 'Lord Oxford'. He wrote several books, including a novel and a brilliant but selective autobiography, and became one of the most successful and influential journalists of his day. He was a friend of many prominent Labour and Liberal politicians, and stood unsuccessfully as a Liberal candidate in Sussex. He later flirted with fascism and in 1934 met Hitler, but failed in his attempt to persuade the Nazi regime to take up test match cricket. He encountered various Prime Ministers from Gladstone to Churchill and, through the influence of his friend Ranjitsinhji, represented India at the League of Nations.

In the 1930s Fry visited Hollywood, hoping for a film career, and met the actors Basil Rathbone and Boris Karloff. Most bizarrely, he was offered the throne of Albania in 1939, but didn't have the necessary £10,000 to accept the post. After suffering a mental breakdown while visiting India, Fry became increasingly eccentric in later life, developing a paranoid fear of Indians and wearing unconventional clothing. He died at the age of 84 in Hampstead, north London.

— HOT (AND COLD) TICKETS —

Over the years England matches have often attracted huge crowds, but none bigger than the 160,000 who crammed into the Maracana stadium in Rio de Janeiro to see the Three Lions take on Brazil on 13th May 1959. Fired on by a passionate home crowd, Brazil won 2–0. At home, England's record attendance is 100,000, the original capacity at the old Wembley stadium. Surprisingly, perhaps, England did not attract a full house at Wembley until 28th November 1951 when Austria were the visitors.

England's lowest home international attendance in the modern era is 15,628 for the friendly against Chile at Wembley on 23rd May 1989. The poor gate was partly explained by a tube strike which made getting to the stadium even more difficult than normal. Yet, by comparison, this was a vast crowd compared to the pitiful turnout of 2,378 who attended England's World Cup qualifier in Bologna against San Marino on 17th November 1993. The fans who stayed away missed a feast of goals as England won 7–1 – but only after San Marino had taken the lead with the fastest ever goal in World Cup history, scored after just nine seconds.

The biggest attendance at an England World Cup game was in 1986 when 114,580 fans watched the infamous quarter-final clash with Argentina in the Azteca stadium, Mexico City. At the other end of the scale, only 5,700 spectators witnessed England's group game with Bulgaria in Rancagua, Chile on 7th June 1962. The fans who decided to give the game a miss didn't miss much, as the match ended in a dull 0–0 draw.

— ENGLAND'S TOP SCORERS —

It is surely only a matter of time before Michael Owen becomes England's record goalscorer. For the moment, though, Sir Bobby Charlton continues to lead the pack as he has done for the past 36 years. At some point in the future Wayne Rooney, too, will almost certainly break into the top ten of all-time England goalscorers, which currently reads:

Player	Caps	Goals
1. **Bobby Charlton** (1958–70)	105	49
2. **Gary Lineker** (1984–92)	80	48
3. **Jimmy Greaves** (1959–67)	57	44
4. **Michael Owen** (1998–)	75	35
5. **Tom Finney** (1946–58)	76	30

6. **Nat Lofthouse** (1950–58)	33	30
7. **Alan Shearer** (1992–2000)	63	30
8. **Viv Woodward** (1903–11)	23	29
9. **Steve Bloomer** (1895–1907)	23	28
10. **David Platt** (1989–96)	62	27

Gary Lineker fluffed a golden opportunity to equal Charlton's England goalscoring record when he dinked a penalty straight at Brazil goalkeeper Carlos at Wembley in May 1992. Having announced that he planned to retire from international football after the European Championships, Lineker travelled to Sweden for the tournament with the nation willing him to score the two goals he needed to set a new record. England, though, played poorly, Lineker barely had a chance and, still one short of Charlton's benchmark, he was surprisingly substituted by boss Graham Taylor in his final international appearance against the hosts.

— ENGLAND AT THE WORLD CUP: 1954 —

Their confidence low after two shattering defeats at the hands of Hungary in recent months, England travelled to Switzerland more in hope than expectation. The squad, though, was an experienced one, with an average age of 29 thanks in part to the presence of Stanley Matthews, still zipping down the wing at the age of 39.

The bizarre format of the tournament, the first to be televised, meant that the two seeded teams in each group would not play each other, only the other two supposedly weaker teams. Thus England avoided a potentially difficult encounter with Italy, and instead were paired with Belgium and the host nation. England's first game against Belgium was a nail-biter, the underdogs coming back from 3–1 down to force extra-time and, eventually, a 4–4 draw. Needing to beat Switzerland to progress to the knock-out stage, England won fairly comfortably thanks to goals by the Wolves duo, Mullen and Wilshaw.

Uruguay, England's opponents in the last eight, were fresh from a 7–0 demolition of Scotland and promised to provide a formidable barrier to the semi-finals. So it proved, as the South Americans ran out 4–2 winners, helped on their way by some poor goalkeeping by Birmingham's Gil Merrick. Still, England had at least improved on their pitiful showing at the previous World Cup four years earlier.

Group table

	P	W	D	L	F	A	Pts
England	2	1	1	0	6	4	3
Italy	2	1	0	1	5	3	2
Switzerland	2	1	0	1	2	3	2
Belgium	2	0	1	1	5	8	1

Date	Venue	Result
17th June 1954	Basel	England 4 Belgium 4*
20th June 1954	Bern	England 2 Switzerland 0
26th June 1954	Basel (Q/F)	England 2 Uruguay 4

* After extra time

England squad: Ivor Broadis (Newcastle, 3 apps), **Roger Byrne** (Manchester United, 3 apps), **Jimmy Dickinson** (Portsmouth, 3 apps), **Tom Finney** (Preston, 3 apps), **Gil Merrick** (Birmingham, 3 apps), **Ron Staniforth** (Huddersfield, 3 apps), **Billy Wright** (Wolves, 3 apps), **Nat Lofthouse** (Bolton, 2 apps), **Stanley Matthews** (Blackpool, 2 apps), **Bill McGarry** (Huddersfield, 2 apps), **Tommy Taylor** (Manchester United, 2 apps), **Dennis Wilshaw** (Wolves, 2 apps), **Jimmy Mullen** (Wolves, 1 app), **Sydney Owen** (Luton, 1 app), **Ken Armstrong*** (Chelsea, 0 apps), **Ted Burgin** (Sheffield United, 0 apps), **Allenby Chilton*** (Manchester United, 0 apps), **Ken Green** (Birmingham City, 0 apps), **Johnny Haynes*** (Fulham, 0 apps), **Harry Hooper** * (West Ham United, 0 apps), **Bedford Jezzard*** (Fulham, 0 apps), **Albert Quixall** (Sheffield Wednesday, 0 apps)
* Did not travel with the squad

Goalscorers: Lofthouse 3, Broadis 2, Mullen 1, Wilshaw 1, own goal 1

Tournament winners: West Germany

They said it

"On his day, Merrick was as good as any, but he was prone to errors we could not afford. He was one of my big mistakes."
England manager **Walter Winterbottom**

"With a bit of luck, we might have reached the semi-finals, because there were long spells when we had Uruguay on the back foot."
Billy Wright, on England's quarter-final exit

"We played well enough in attack, but were woefully weak in defence and midfield."
Stanley Matthews

— BAD HAIR DAY XI —

A team of England internationals sporting dubious hairstyles:

1. **David Seaman** (St. Trinian's-style ponytail)
2. **Rio Ferdinand** (Birds' nest afro)
3. **Danny Mills** (Fan-in-the-stands slaphead)
4. **Trevor Cherry** (Oompah Loompah gone wrong)
5. **Kevin Keegan** (Absurd bubble perm)
6. **Bryan Robson** (Even more absurd bubble perm)
7. **David Beckham** (Take your pick: spiky quiff to flowing locks strapped under girly Alice band)
8. **Peter Beardsley** (Inmate-in-an-asylum jagged bowl cut)
9. **Bobby Charlton** (Wispy strands combed over increasingly bald pate)
10. **Brian Little** (Mid-70s hippy mane with unfeasibly high fringe)
11. **Chris Waddle** (Kajagoogoo-style 80s mullet)

Barnet FC . . . Keegan, Seaman, Waddle and Beckham

— HE'S MY BROTHER —

A total of 20 sets of brothers have played for England, the most famous being 1966 World Cup winners Bobby and Jack Charlton and their latterday (although somewhat less successful) equivalents, Gary and Phil Neville. Of this score of soccer siblings, ten played together in the same England team and they are:

Brothers	Caps won together	Years played together
Gary and Phil Neville*	31	1996–2004
Bobby and Jack Charlton	28	1965–70
Arthur and Percy Walters	9	1885–89
Frank and Frederick Forman	3	1889
Arthur and Edward Bambridge^	2	1883–84
Arthur and Henry Cursham	2	1883
Herbert and William Rawson	1	1875
Charles and Hubert Heron	1	1876
Frederick and John Hargreaves	1	1881
Arthur and Robert Topham	1	1894

*Gary and Phil's sister, Tracey, has also won 75 caps for England at netball
^Another brother, Ernest Bambridge, played one match for England in 1876

— ENGLAND LEGENDS: SIR STANLEY MATTHEWS —

Arguably still the most famous England international of all time, Stanley Matthews was a twinkle-toed winger who could skip past defenders as if they weren't there. Not for nothing was he known as 'the Wizard of the Dribble', a nickname which perfectly summed up his bewitching skills.

Matthews tormented international defences for an incredible 23 years, after winning his first cap against Wales at the age of 19 in 1934. In the pre-war years he produced some of his greatest performances for England, scoring a hat-trick against Czechoslovakia at White Hart Lane in 1937 and reducing 100,000 swastika-waving German fans to silence as England swept to a stunning 6–3 victory over Germany in Berlin the following year.

After the war, Matthews continued to dazzle in an England shirt, playing for his country until the ripe old age of 41. His final caps tally of 54 could easily have been doubled if he hadn't been overlooked so often by the selectors, some of whom felt that he was too individual a player.

The fans, though, adored him and there was a public outcry when he was not recalled one last time for the 1958 World Cup. Incredibly Matthews, by then 43 but still as fit as ever thanks to his strict training regime, carried on playing in league football for another seven years before finally retiring at the age of 50 in 1965. That same year his remarkable career was crowned with a knighthood.

Sir Stanley Matthews Factfile
Born: Stoke, 1st February 1915 **Died:** 23rd February 2000
Clubs: Stoke City, Blackpool
Caps: 54 (1934–57)
Goals: 11
England debut: Wales 0 England 4, 29th September 1934

Others on Matthews

"Stan used to put the ball on my centre-parting. They don't do that anymore."

Former England centre-forward **Tommy Lawton**, 1985

"Even at 42, there were many who considered his England career had been finished too early. Just his name on the teamsheet would have given us a psychological advantage."

Billy Wright

'The Wizard of Dribble'

— ALF'S 007 MISSION —

The day after England began their 1966 World Cup campaign with a frustrating 0–0 draw against an ultra-defensive Uruguay, Alf Ramsey sought to lighten the mood by taking his squad to Pinewood Studios to meet the cast of the James Bond film *Thunderball*.

Among the famous names the players encountered on the set were Yul Brynner, Britt Ekland and Cliff Richard and, of course, Sean Connery. Even the normally unflappable Ramsey became quite excited when he spotted the Bond actor, shouting out, "Look lads, it's Sean Connery!" Unfortunately, he pronounced 'Sean' as 'seen' – a boob that led to much laughter and prompted England captain Bobby Moore to put his arm round Ramsey and say, "Now I've shorn everything!"

The players returned to their hotel in Hendon in much better spirits and a few days later beat Mexico in their second game. As the tournament continued Ramsey took his team on further group outings, to see a western film and Ken Dodd live on stage. So, bizarre though it sounds, you could say that Bond, cowboys and the Diddymen all played their part in England's eventual triumph.

—YANKEE DOODLE NOT SO DANDY —

England have suffered some shocking defeats in their time, but surely none as humiliating as the 1–0 loss to the USA at the 1950 World Cup. England, competing in the tournament for the first time, were one of the favourites for the trophy and in players like Stanley Matthews, Tom Finney and Wilf Mannion possessed some of the most famous names in the world game. The Americans, on the other, had no such pedigree and were captained by a Glaswegian, Eddie McIlvenney, who had been given a free transfer by lowly Wrexham three years earlier.

England were expected to win comfortably, but instead lost to a 37th minute header by Haiti-born Larry Gaetjaens. Despite furious English pressure the equaliser just wouldn't come and, at the final whistle, the victorious Americans were carried shoulder high off the pitch.

The defeat has gone down in history as England's most embarrassing ever but, as centre forward Roy Bentley later explained, there were some extenuating circumstances:

> *"It was like a Sunday league game. There weren't any showers and we changed in the school next door. The pitch was awful but they never had the grounds for the World Cup. The main stadium over there took all the money that was needed for the rest.*
> *In the game we must have hit the woodwork half a dozen*

times. I hit it three times, one with a shot, two with headers. Their goalkeeper dived into Tom Finney as though he were making a rugby tackle. It should have been a penalty. But upsets happen in football."

The England players were never allowed to forget the defeat and nor was the manager, Walter Winterbottom, who recalled:

"When I returned to the States, they were determined to remind me of that day. They presented me with an enlarged 'colour' photograph of the winning goal . . . they'd actually painted a black and white picture."

— THREE LIONS ON A SHIRT —

The badge of the England football team combines three lions and nine red-and-white Tudor roses. Three lions have been a national symbol of England since the twelfth century when Richard 1st (Richard the Lionheart) adopted the Lions of Anjou – a symbol of the Norman power from which he was descended – for his coat of arms. Tudor roses, meanwhile, are another common English national image, originally symbolising the end of the Wars of the Roses in 1485.

The England team badge itself dates back to 1872 when a version of it appeared on the the national team's white shirts for the country's first ever international against Scotland.

The badge has since undergone a number of redesigns, the most radical of which saw the original crown above the lions disappear in 1949. In 2003 a gold star, signifying England's World Cup victory in 1966, appeared on the sleeve of the players' shirts after a campaign by the TV show *Soccer AM* but, in line with the practice adopted by other countries that have won the competition, it has since been moved to a position above the national badge.

England's badge is shared with the Football Association, but is not to be confused with the crest of Shrewsbury Town FC, which also features three lions.

Shield courtesy of www.spiral.org.uk

— THE LONG AND THE SHORT OF IT —

The gangling Peter Crouch is the tallest player to ever appear for England. The Liverpool striker stands a remarkable 6 ft 7 in his socks, a full 15 inches taller than the shortest player to represent England, Fanny Walden. The Tottenham winger, who made his international debut in 1914 before winning his second and final cap in 1922, was reportedly just 5 ft 2 in tall.

— ENGLAND AT THE WORLD CUP: 1958 —

But for the Munich Air Disaster of February 1958, England might well have won the World Cup held in Sweden four months later. But, without the talismanic Duncan Edwards, centre forward Tommy Taylor and left-back Roger Byrne, all of whom were among the Manchester United players who perished in the accident, Walter Winterbottom's patched-up side were never going to have more than an outside chance of success in a strong field.

Drawn in a tough group which included eventual winners Brazil, Olympic champions the Soviet Union and the formidable Austrians, England got off to a reasonable start with a gutsy 2–2 draw against a physical Russian side. Another draw with the talented Brazilians put England in a good position in the group, but a third stalemate against already eliminated Austria meant they would have to meet Russia again in a play-off to decide who would go through to the quarter-finals.

Despite making three changes to his team for the decider, Winterbottom resisted a press campaign to play Manchester United's 20-year-old winger Bobby Charlton, who remained on the bench. England had the better of the match against the Soviets, but lost 1–0 and, frustratingly, returned home from the tournament before both Wales and Northern Ireland.

Group table

	P	W	D	L	F	A	Pts
Brazil	3	2	1	0	5	0	5
England	3	0	3	0	4	4	3
Russia	3	1	1	1	4	4	3
Austria	3	0	1	2	2	7	1

Date	Venue	Result
8th June 1958	Gothenburg	England 2 USSR 2
11th June 1958	Gothenburg	England 0 Brazil 0
15th June 1958	Boras	England 2 Austria 2
17th June 1958	Gothenburg (Play-off)	England 0 USSR 1

England squad: Tom Banks (Bolton, 4 apps), **Johnny Haynes** (Fulham, 4 apps), **Don Howe** (WBA, 4 apps), **Derek Kevan** (WBA, 4 apps), **Colin McDonald** (Burnley, 4 apps), **Bill Slater** (Wolves, 4 apps), **Billy Wright** (Wolves, 4 apps), **Alan A'Court** (Liverpool, 3 apps), **Ed Clamp** (Wolves, 3 apps), **Bryan Douglas** (Blackburn, 3 apps), **Bobby Robson** (WBA, 3 apps), **Peter Brabrook** (Chelsea, 1 app), **Peter Broadbent** (Wolves, 1 app), **Ronnie Clayton** (Blackburn, 1 app), **Tom Finney** (Preston, 1 app), **Bobby Charlton** (Manchester United, 0 apps), **Alan Hodgkinson*** (Sheffield United, 0 apps), **Ed Hopkinson** (Bolton, 0 apps), **Maurice Norman** (Tottenham, 0 apps), **Maurice Setters*** (WBA, 0 apps), **Peter Sillett** (Chelsea, 0 apps), **Bobby Smith** (Tottenham, 0 apps)
* Did not travel with the squad

Goalscorers: Kevan 2, Finney 1, Haynes 1

Tournament winners: Brazil

They said it

"The Russians fouled a lot, something we hadn't expected."

Don Howe on England's group opponents

"England could not be faulted for effort or commitment during the '58 World Cup . . . but our technical ability left a lot to be desired."

Tom Finney

"When we arrived back in England, Walter Winterbottom was met at the airport by his young son, Alan, who asked the question on the lips of thousands of football fans: 'Daddy, why didn't you play Bobby Charlton?'"

Billy Wright

— THE GOD SQUAD —

You wouldn't really expect to see the Archbishop of Canterbury, the Archbishop of Westminster or the Chief Rabbi lining up for England, but in days gone by it was not unknown for the national team to feature a man of the cloth. Indeed, no fewer than seven reverends have pulled on an England shirt and they are:

Rev. Arnold Smith (1 cap, 1872)
Rev. Robert Vidal (1 cap, 1873)
Rev. John Owen (1 cap, 1874)
Rev. Beaumont Jarrett (3 caps, 1876–78)
Rev. Edward Lyttleton (1 cap, 1878)
Rev. Francis Pawson (2 caps, 1883–85)
Rev. Kenneth Hunt (2 caps, 1911)

Not quite a whole team there, but throw in Sidney Bishop (4 caps, 1927), Edward Christian (1 cap, 1879), Alfred Priest (1 cap, 1900) and legendary striker Dixie Dean (16 caps, 1927–33) and you've got a complete side full of (Holy) spirit.

— ENGLAND LEGENDS: BILLY WRIGHT —

The first player in the world to win 100 caps, Billy Wright was the lynchpin of the England defence throughout the 1950s. A fine reader of the game and a good tackler, he was also strong in the air despite not being especially tall.

Wright captained England at three World Cups, although none of the tournaments were particularly successful. In 1950 he was part of the team that surprisingly lost to the USA, and he again had to raise the morale of his team-mates following heavy defeats by the powerful Hungarians in 1953 and 1954. Unusually, Wright's last game before retirement was an international, an 8–1 victory over USA in Los Angeles in May 1959. He went on to manage Arsenal for four years during the 1960s and was later in charge of the England under-23 and youth teams.

A gentleman on and off the pitch, Wright was never booked while playing for England. Always a favourite with the fans, his popularity soared even higher when he married pop singer Joy Beverley. The couple were the Posh and Becks of their day – but without the whacky clothes, the strangely-named children or the X-rated text messages.

Billy Wright Factfile
Born: Ironbridge, 6th February 1924 **Died:** 3rd September 1994
Club: Wolves
Caps: 105 (1947–59)
Goals: 3
England debut: England 1 Scotland 1, 12th April 1947
International honours: England captain 90 times (1948–59)

Others on Wright

"He gave everything he had every time he went on the pitch, and was an inspiration to all his team-mates."

Sir Stanley Matthews

"After his 100th cap, Ronnie Clayton and I hoisted him up and carried him the length of the pitch and into the dressing-room. He was so modest that he wanted us to put him down, but we insisted he stay up there."

Wright's England team-mate **Don Howe**

Billy Wright – "an inspiration"

— CAN WE PLAY YOU EVERY WEEK? —

Mention the word 'Poland' to most England fans over the age of 40 and they'll probably grimace. That's because thirty odd years ago the Poles put England out of the 1974 World Cup at the qualifying stage, and ever since the Eastern Europeans have been deemed something of a bogey side for our boys. In fact, nothing could be further from the truth. In 14 meetings between the countries since Poland triumphed 2–0 in Chorzow in June 1973, England have won nine and drawn five – the Three Lions' longest undefeated run against any country in the world at the present time.

That sequence, impressive though it is, is still some way from being a record. Between 1883 and 1914 England remained unbeaten in 32 matches against Wales while Ireland didn't beat England until 1913 – after 31 previous attempts dating back to 1882.

— CAPLESS IN CARDIFF —

Among the 44 clubs in the top two flights of English football at the start of the 2005/06 season, the following four are yet to provide an England international:

Cardiff City
Hull City
Plymouth Argyle
Wigan Athletic

— THRASHED BY ALIENS! —

England's worst ever defeat occurred on 23rd May 1954 when they were tonked 7–1 by Hungary in Budapest. "The Hungarians are from another planet," was the considered verdict of *The Daily Mail*. The margin of the reverse was a shock, but not a complete surprise as the Hungarians had won 6–3 at Wembley only six months previously. England's heaviest defeats, including the Budapest debacle, are as follows:

Date	Venue	Result
23rd May 1954	Budapest	Hungary 7 England 1
2nd March 1878	Glasgow	Scotland 7 England 2
12th March 1881	Kennington	England 1 Scotland 6
11th May 1958	Belgrade	Yugoslavia 5 England 0
11th March 1882	Glasgow	Scotland 5 England 1
31th March 1928	Wembley	England 1 Scotland 5
30th May 1964	Rio de Janeiro	Brazil 5 England 1

— SIX SAINTS SKIPPERS —

In the calendar year 1982 no fewer than six players who had either captained England, or would do so in the future, played for Southampton. The players (with the number of times they captained England in brackets) were:

Alan Ball (6)
Mick Channon (2)
Kevin Keegan (31)
Mick Mills (8)
Peter Shilton (15)
Dave Watson (3)

— A NUTTY NORWEGIAN —

On 9th September 1981 England sensationally lost a World Cup qualifying match against Norway in Oslo, putting their hopes of qualifying for the finals in Spain in considerable doubt. Norway had lost all five of their previous games against England so, understandably, the home fans were ecstatic when the match ended. None more so than Norwegian radio commentator Borge Lillelien, who regaled his listeners with these famous words:

> *"There! He blew the whistle! Norway has beaten England 2–1 at football and we are the best in the world! England, the home of the giants! Lord Nelson, Lord Beaverbrook, Sir Winston Churchill, Sir Anthony Eden, Clement Attlee, Henry Cooper, Lady Diana . . . [rambles for a few seconds in Norwegian] . . . Can you hear me Maggie Thatcher? Your boys took one hell of a beating. Your boys took one hell of a beating!"*

Some readers, younger ones especially, may not be familiar with all the names mentioned by the over-excitable Lillelien, so here's an explanatory cast list:

Lord Nelson English Admiral and hero of the Battle of Trafalgar (1758–1805)

Lord Beaverbrook British newspaper proprietor and Conservative politician (1879–1964)

Sir Winston Churchill British Prime Minister during World War II (1874–1965)

Sir Anthony Eden British Prime Minister in the 1950s (1897–1977)

Clement Attlee British Prime minister after World War II (1883–1967)

Henry Cooper British heavyweight boxer (1934–)

Lady Diana (or **Princess Diana** as she was then) Wife of HRH Prince Charles (1961–97)

Maggie (**Margaret**) **Thatcher** British Prime Minister of the 1980s (1925–)

— IF THE CAP FITS . . . —

England international caps were first awarded in 1886, and to this day players picked for the Three Lions are presented with a hand-made 'cap'. The original England caps were royal blue and featured a rose emblem. Later the rose was changed to the more familiar three lions emblem, other colours were added and a tassel was attached to the cap.

In 1959 Billy Wright became the first England player to win 100 caps, and he went on to finish with 105. However, Wright's collection of actual caps only stood at 93 as, from 1953 onwards, players were awarded a tournament cap for the British Home Championship rather than one for each game.

England caps are made by a company called Toye, Kenning and Spencer, who also produce mayor's chains, medals and Masonic regalia.

— ENGLAND AT THE WORLD CUP: 1962 —

Installed high in the Andes in the Chilean mining town of Rancagua, England set up camp in a site normally used as a rest centre for executives of an American copper company. Although the complex featured tennis courts and a golf course, there were no television sets and the players amused themselves in the evenings by telling stories and reading. To complete the spartan picture, some players were billeted in miners' shacks complete with corrugated roofs.

England opened their campaign with a disappointing 2–1 defeat to a Hungarian side which was not a patch on the 'Magical Magyars' of the previous decade. Virtually written off by the press, England responded with a vastly improved performance against Argentina two days later against to record a victory which revived their hopes of qualification.

Needing just a point in their last match to reach the knockout stage, England ground out a dull 0–0 draw with their already eliminated opponents, Bulgaria. The performance, though, was far from impressive with star names like skipper Johnny Haynes and goal poacher extraordinaire Jimmy Greaves looking jaded.

England's failure to top their group meant they were paired in the quarter-finals with tournament favourites and World Cup holders Brazil. In a Jekyll and Hyde campaign, Walter Winterbottom's side put on their finest display of the competition, but still went down to a 3–1 defeat largely inspired by brilliant Brazilian winger Garrincha.

Group table

	P	W	D	L	F	A	Pts
Hungary	3	2	1	0	8	2	5
England	3	1	1	1	4	3	3
Argentina	3	1	1	1	2	3	3
Bulgaria	3	0	1	2	1	7	1

Date	Venue	Result
31st May 1962	Rancagua	England 1 Hungary 2
2nd June 1962	Rancagua	England 3 Argentina 1
7th June 1962	Rancagua	England 0 Bulgaria 0
10th June 1962	Vina del Mar (Q/F)	England 1 Brazil 3

England squad: Jimmy Armfield (Blackpool, 4 apps), **Bobby Charlton** (Manchester United, 4 apps), **Bryan Douglas** (Blackburn, 4 apps), **Ron Flowers** (Wolves, 4 apps), **Jimmy Greaves** (Tottenham, 4 apps), **Johnny Haynes** (Fulham, 4 apps), **Bobby Moore** (West Ham, 4 apps), **Maurice Norman** (Tottenham, 4 apps), **Ron Springett** (Sheffield Wednesday, 4 apps), **Ray Wilson** (Huddersfield, 4 apps), **Gerry Hitchens** (Inter Milan, 2 apps), **Alan Peacock**, (Middlesbrough, 2 apps), **Jimmy Adamson** (Burnley, 0 apps), **Stanley Anderson** (Sunderland, 0 apps), **John Connelly** (Burnley, 0 apps), **George Eastham** (Arsenal, 0 apps), **Alan Hodgkinson** (Sheffield United, 0 apps), **Don Howe** (WBA, 0 apps), **Roger Hunt** (Liverpool, 0 apps), **Derek Kevan*** (WBA, 0 apps), **Bobby Robson** (WBA, 0 apps), **Peter Swan** (Sheffield Wednesday, 0 apps)

* Did not travel with squad

Goalscorers: Flowers 2, Charlton 1, Greaves 1, Hitchens 1

Winners: Brazil

They said it

"I felt there was no disgrace in England's 3–1 defeat at the hands of the Brazilians. Brazil were far and away the best team in that World Cup."

Jimmy Greaves

"Garrincha walked like a cripple, which I suppose he was, but he was even quicker off the mark than Stan Matthews in his heyday."

Johnny Haynes on Brazil's star player,
who had suffered from polio in childhood

"We could have done a lot better, you know. Even against Brazil we missed chances before they put the game beyond our reach."

Walter Winterbottom

— A CUP'S A CUP —

Over the years England have won a number of minor cups and tournaments. Although these victories have not quite got the fans dancing in the streets they have, nonetheless been welcome – especially in the absence, since 1966, of more serious silverware:

Date	Venue	Tournament	Opponents
April 1986	Wembley	Rous Cup	Scotland
May 1988	Wembley	Rous Cup	Scotland, Colombia
May 1989	Wembley/ Hampden	Rous Cup	Chile, Scotland
May 1991	Wembley	England Challenge Cup	USSR, Argentina
June 1997	France (various)	Tournoi de France	France, Italy, Brazil
June 2004	City of Manchester Stadium	FA Summer Tournament	Japan, Iceland

— MOORO TOPS ALL-TIME POLL —

In November 2003 the official FA website, **www.thefa.com**, invited fans to vote for the greatest England player of the previous 50 years. Perhaps unsurprisingly, 1966 World Cup-winning skipper Bobby Moore topped the poll with an impressive 50% of all votes cast. Less predictably, 1950s striker Nat Lofthouse came second (18%) following an organised internet campaign by Bolton fans. Sir Bobby Charlton was third with 10% of the votes. The top ten in full read:

1. **Bobby Moore**
2. **Nat Lofthouse**
3. **Sir Bobby Charlton**
4. **David Beckham**
5. **Sir Stanley Matthews**
6. **Alan Shearer**
7. **Gary Lineker**
8. **Paul Gascoigne**
9. **Jimmy Greaves**
10. **Kevin Keegan**

— ALF RAMSEY'S FIRST ENGLAND TEAM —

Destined to become his country's greatest manager, Alf Ramsey's reign as England boss got off to the worst possible start with a 5–2 defeat away to France on 27th February 1963. The team the former championship-winning manager of Ipswich chose included just two players – Bobby Moore and Bobby Charlton – who would go on to achieve football immortality by winning the World Cup three years later. Here's Ramsey's first side in full:

1. **Ron Springett** (Sheffield Wednesday)
2. **Jimmy Armfield** (Blackpool, captain)
3. **Ron Henry** (Tottenham)
4. **Bobby Moore** (West Ham United)
5. **Brian Labone** (Everton)
6. **Ron Flowers** (Wolves)
7. **John Connelly** (Burnley)
8. **Bobby Tambling** (Chelsea)
9. **Bobby Smith** (Tottenham)
10. **Jimmy Greaves** (Tottenham)
10. **Bobby Charlton** (Manchester United)

— 1966: 'I WAS THERE!' —

Mike Crisp from Hornchurch, Essex, was lucky enough to be present at the 1966 World Cup final between England and West Germany. In an interview with **www.bbc.co.uk** he described his experiences on the day:

> *"I stood in the north-east corner of Wembley, close to a Brazilian who turned up with a drum to offer support to England. It was him who provided the now famous beat: Bang bang! Bang bang bang! Bang bang bang bang! To which everyone responded: 'England!'*
>
> *Every time West Germany attacked it was like a knife in the stomach. I did enjoy it, but I was like a piece of limp rag at the end. When the final whistle blew it was the first time in my life I embraced a complete stranger. It was a magic moment that I hope will be repeated, but so far, except perhaps 1990, it's never looked like happening again."*

— ANIMAL MAGIC XI —

Yes, it's enough to get Sir David Attenborough dashing off to the new Wembley – a team of England players drawn from the natural world:

1. **Frank Swift** (19 caps, 1947–49)
2. **Hubert Heron** (5 caps, 1873–78)
3. **Robert Gosling** (5 caps, 1892–95)
4. **Peter Swan** (19 caps, 1960–62)
5. **Alvin Martin** (17 caps, 1981–86)
6. **Thelwell Pike** (1 cap, 1886)
7. **Alan Peacock** (6 caps, 1962–65)
8. **Steve Bull** (13 caps, 1989–90)
9. **Ted Drake** (5 caps, 1935–38)
10. **Tony Woodcock** (42 caps, 1978–86)
11. **Steve Guppy** (1 cap, 1999)

— NIGHTMARES, SHOCKERS AND TURNIPS —

The 10 most humiliating defeats in England's history . . .

No.	Date	Venue	Result
1	29th June 1950	Belo Horizante	England 0 USA 1
2	9th Sept 1981	Oslo	Norway 2 England 1
3	25th Nov 1953	Wembley	England 3 Hungary 6
4	7th Sept 2005	Belfast	N. Ireland 1 England 0
5	31th March 1928	Wembley	England 1 Scotland 5
6	9th June 1993	Boston	USA 2 England 0
7	12th Feb 2003	Upton Park	England 1 Australia 3
8	17th May 1980	Wrexham	Wales 4 England 1
9	2nd June 1993	Oslo	Norway 2 England 0
10	17th Aug 2005	Copenhagen	Denmark 4 England 1

— ENGLAND'S FIRST GOAL —

With England's first ever match away to Scotland in 1872 ending in a 0–0 draw, it wasn't until the return fixture with the Scots the following year that the Three Lions managed to find the net for the first time in the country's history.

Happily, fans at the Kennington Oval didn't have long to wait before they were throwing their hats in the air as William Kenyon-Slaney of Wanderers FC scored after just one minute. As was the custom at the time after a goal, the sides immediately swapped ends.

Kenyon-Slaney added a second goal after half-time as England won 4–2 to record the first ever victory in international football.

Born in Rajkot, India, Kenyon-Slaney was a captain in the Household Brigade who later became an MP. Apart from scoring England's first goal, he also has the distinction of being the first player born outside the UK to win an international cap.

— ENGLAND LEGENDS: BOBBY MOORE —

Bobby Moore will forever be remembered as the captain of England's 1966 World Cup-winning team. Even now, four decades on, the image of Moore being held aloft by his team-mates on the Wembley pitch while clutching the Jules Rimet trophy remains one of the most iconic in British sport.

A cool and composed central defender, Moore was a tremendous reader of the game – an asset which made up for his lack of pace. His intuitive understanding of the game made him a natural captain, a role he performed for England on 90 occasions to equal Billy Wright's record. Apart from his heroics in 1966 when he was voted Player of the Tournament, Moore also appeared at the 1962 World Cup and was still captain when England defended their trophy in Mexico in 1970. Having being falsely accused of stealing a bracelet en route to the tournament, Moore might have been excused some under par performances; instead, he was at the top of his game, arguably putting in his finest ever display in an England shirt in the 1–0 defeat by eventual champions Brazil. A superbly-timed block tackle on Brazilian striker Jairzinho, followed by a perfectly delivered pass out of defence, summed up Moore's magnificent contribution to a legendary match.

Moore's final appearances for his country were less memorable. A costly mistake in Poland in June 1973 led to a defeat which helped scupper England's hopes of qualifying for the 1974 World Cup, and by the time of his final and record-setting 108th cap he was clearly past his best. Far better to remember Moore in his prime, striking a superb long pass for Geoff Hurst to score his hat-trick goal in the World Cup final and then, minutes later, thoughtfully wiping his dirty hands before collecting football's most coveted trophy from The Queen.

Bobby Moore Factfile
Born: Barking, 12th April 1941 **Died:** 24th February 1993
Club: West Ham United, Fulham
Caps: 108 (1962–73)

Goals: 2
England debut: Peru 0 England 4, 20th May 1962
International honours: England captain 90 times (1963–73), World Cup winner 1966

Others on Moore

"Mooro didn't shout; he left that to big Jack, Ray and me. He led, minute by minute, second by second, by sheer example."

Nobby Stiles

"Someone would come and kick a lump out of him, and he'd play as though he hadn't noticed. But ten minutes later . . . whoof! . . . he had a great 'golden boy' image. But he was hard."

Geoff Hurst

Bobby Moore: Legend

— WORLD CUP WINNERS HONOURED —

England's 1966 World Cup-winning heroes have now all received Royal Honours, although almost half the side had to wait for their gongs until 2000 – some 33 years after Alf Ramsey became 'Sir Alf' and Bobby Moore collected his OBE. The team's various honours are:

Team member	Honour
Sir Alf Ramsey	Knighthood (1967)
Bobby Moore	OBE (1967)
Sir Bobby Charlton	OBE (1969), CBE (1974), Knighthood (1994)
Gordon Banks	OBE (1970)
Jack Charlton	OBE (1974)
Martin Peters	MBE (1978)
Sir Geoff Hurst	MBE (1979), Knighthood (1998)
Alan Ball	MBE (2000)
George Cohen	MBE (2000)
Roger Hunt	MBE (2000)
Nobby Stiles	MBE (2000)
Ray Wilson	MBE (2000)

— YOUNG GUNS, OLD STAGERS —

Wayne Rooney became England's youngest ever player when he came on at half-time against Australia at Upton Park on 12th February 2003 at the tender age of 17 years and 111 days. Most newspapers reported that the young striker beat a record previously held by Michael Owen but, in fact, the youngest England debutante before Rooney was James Prinsep of Clapham Rovers, who was aged 17 years and 253 days when he played against Scotland on 5th April 1879.

Rooney is also England's youngest goalscorer, striking against Macedonia in Skopje on 6th September 2003 aged 17 years and 317 days. This time, the record he broke was previously held by Michael Owen who was aged 18 and 147 days when he was on target against Morocco in Casablanca shortly before the start of the 1998 World Cup.

The youngest player to captain England is Bobby Moore, who was aged 22 and 48 days when he first wore the armband against Czechoslovakia in Bratislava on 29th May 1963. Moore, who was to go on to captain his country another 89 times, got off to a winning start as skipper as England recorded an impressive 4–2 away victory.

The oldest player to turn out for England is twinkle-toed winger Stanley Matthews. 'The Wizard of the Dribble' was aged 42 and 104 days when he played his final international match against Denmark in Copenhagen on 15th May 1957. Unsurprisingly, Matthews is also the oldest England scorer, finding the net against Northern Ireland in 1956 aged 41 and 248 days.

The oldest player to make his debut for England is Leslie Compton of Arsenal. He was aged 38 and two months when he won the first of his two caps in a 4–2 victory over Wales at Roker Park on 15th November 1950.

— WINNING RUN —

Way back in 1908–09 England put together their best ever winning run of ten consecutive victories. The sequence began with a 6–1 thrashing of Austria in Vienna in June 1908 and finally came to an end 20 months later, when they were held to a 1–1 draw by Ireland in Belfast. During the run, the Three Lions rattled up an incredible total of 56 goals while conceding just seven in reply. The results during this purple patch were:

Date	Venue	Result
6th June 1908	Vienna	Austria 1 England 6
8th June 1908	Vienna	Austria 1 England 11
10th June 1908	Budapest	Hungary 0 England 7
13th June 1908	Prague	Bohemia 0 England 4
13th Feb 1909	Bradford	England 4 Ireland 0
15th Mar 1909	Nottingham	England 2 Wales 0
3rd April 1909	Crystal Palace	England 2 Scotland 0
29th May 1909	Budapest	Hungary 2 England 4
31st May 1909	Budapest	Hungary 2 England 8
1st June 1909	Vienna	Austria 1 England 8

— TIME GENTLEMEN, PLEASE —

Dozens of England internationals have gone on to run a pub or bar after their football careers finished. Here are just a few:

Charlie George (1 cap, 1976) The Ashley Hotel, Hampshire
Bobby Moore (108 caps, 1962–73) The Black Bull, Stratford
Peter Osgood (4 caps, 1970–73) Old Union pub, Windsor
Carlton Palmer (18 caps, 1992–93) Dam House Bar & Restaurant, Sheffield
Alan Sunderland (1 cap, 1980) The Halberd Inn, Ipswich
Terry Venables (2 caps, 1964) Scribes West, Kensington

— ENGLAND AT THE WORLD CUP: 1966 —

Hosting the World Cup for the first time, England went into the 1966 tournament as one of the favourites, the expectation of the nation intensified by manager Alf Ramsey's bold prediction that his side would win the competition.

Few shared Ramsey's confidence after a disappointing 0–0 draw in the opening match with Uruguay, but a trademark Bobby Charlton thunderbolt against Mexico finally got England going. Victory over the central Americans was followed by another comfortable win over France, although an ugly tackle by midfield enforcer Nobby Stiles led to press demands for the Manchester United player to be dropped from the team. Typically, Ramsey defended Stiles, telling the FA blazers, "If he goes, I go." Neither of them did.

In the quarter-final England struggled to break down an uncompromising Argentina side, even after the dismissal of their captain, Antonio Rattin. Eventually, Geoff Hurst, deputising for the injured Jimmy Greaves, headed the winner from a perfect cross by his West Ham team-mate Martin Peters. At the final whistle, a furious Ramsey refused to let his players swap shirts with their opponents before describing the Argentineans as 'animals' in the post-match press conference. England-Argentina meetings have had a distinct edge to them ever since.

The semi-final was a happier affair. England's opponents, Portugal, had been indebted to their star player, the lithe Eusebio, in coming from three goals down to beat North Korea 5–3 in the quarter-finals. But with Stiles keeping a close watch on 'The Black Pearl', England won more comfortably than the 2–1 scoreline suggests, Bobby Charlton hitting both goals for the home side.

So to the final against West Germany, conquerors of Russia in the other semi-final. On a sunny day interrupted by occasional light showers and in front of a worldwide TV audience of 500 million, England got off to a poor start, going a goal down when a weak headed clearance by Ray Wilson was drilled home by Helmut Haller. Minutes later, however, Ramsey's decision to persist with Hurst rather than recall Greaves was vindicated when the centre forward headed skipper Bobby Moore's beautifully flighted free kick past the German goalkeeper, Tilkowski.

A closely fought match appeared to be heading England's way when Martin Peters scored from close range with just 12 minutes left, but a scrappy German equalizer almost on full-time cut short the home fans' celebrations. In the first half of extra time Hurst crashed a fierce shot against the underside of the bar, the ball bounced down either on or over the line and, after consulting the Russian linesman, the referee awarded a goal. It was Hurst, too, who confirmed England's triumph in the closing seconds with a rasping drive into the roof of the German net, making him the first – and so far only – player to score a hat-trick in the World Cup final.

Group table

	P	W	D	L	F	A	Pts
England	3	2	1	0	4	0	5
Uruguay	3	1	2	0	2	1	4
Mexico	3	0	2	1	1	3	2
France	3	0	1	2	2	5	1

Date	Venue	Result
11th July 1966	Wembley	England 0 Uruguay 0
16th July 1966	Wembley	England 2 Mexico 0
20th July 1966	Wembley	England 2 France 0
23rd July 1966	Wembley (Q/F)	England 1 Argentina 0
26th July 1966	Wembley (S/F)	England 2 Portugal 1
30th July 1966	Wembley (Final)	England 4 West Germany 2*

* After extra time

England squad: Gordon Banks (Leicester City, 6 apps), **Bobby Charlton** (Manchester United, 6 apps), **Jack Charlton** (Leeds United, 6 apps), **George Cohen** (Fulham, 6 apps), **Roger Hunt** (Liverpool, 6 apps), **Bobby Moore** (West Ham United, 6 apps), **Nobby Stiles** (6 apps), **Ray Wilson** (Everton, 6 apps), **Martin Peters** (West Ham United, 5 apps), **Alan Ball** (Blackpool, 4 apps), **Jimmy Greaves** (Tottenham, 3 apps), **Geoff Hurst** (West Ham United, 3 apps), **Ian Callaghan** (Liverpool, 1 app), **John Connelly** (Manchester United, 1 app), **Terry Paine** (Southampton, 1 app), **Jimmy Armfield** (Blackpool, 0 apps), **Peter Bonetti** (Chelsea, 0 apps), **Gerry Byrne** (Liverpool, 0 apps), **George Eastham** (Arsenal, 0 apps), **Ron Flowers** (Wolves, 0 apps), **Norman Hunter** (Leeds United, 0 apps), **Ron Springett** (Sheffield Wednesday, 0 apps)

Goalscorers: Hurst 4, Charlton 3, Hunt 3, Peters 1

Tournament winners: England

They said it

"England's best football will come against the right type of opposition – a team who come to play football and not act as animals."

England manager **Alf Ramsey** after his side's battling quarter-final win over Argentina

"You've beaten them once. Now go out and bloody beat them again."
Alf Ramsey to his weary players before the start of
extra-time in the World Cup final

"Some managers are tactically aware. Some excel at coaching. Others are
good at motivation and man management. Alf was superb at everything."
England goalkeeper **Gordon Banks**

"I have to admit that I had a bit of sympathy for the Germans. They
genuinely believed that the ball had not crossed the line and they may
be right."
Scorer **Geoff Hurst** on England's controversial
third goal in the World Cup final

"The Queen enjoyed it enormously, and was thrilled during the final
part of extra time. She kept asking, 'How much longer to go?'"
Sir Stanley Rous, President of FIFA,
who was sat next to The Queen at the final

"I said that it would take a great side to beat us because we are a
great side."

Alf Ramsey's post-victory verdict

England: 1966 World Champions

— WORLD CUP STALWARTS —

England's leading appearance makers in World Cup finals matches are:

Peter Shilton, 17 apps (1982–90)
Terry Butcher, 14 apps (1982–90)
Bobby Charlton, 14 apps (1958–70)
Bobby Moore, 14 apps (1962–70)
Gary Lineker, 12 apps (1986–90)

— FOUR WHO GOT FIVE —

Just four players have scored five goals in a match for England. The last striker to achieve this feat was Newcastle favourite Malcolm 'Supermac' Macdonald who scored all five of England's goals against Cyprus in a European Championship qualifier at Wembley in April 1975. The full list of players sharing this particular record is:

Player	Goals	Date	Venue	Match result
Oliver Vaughton	5	18th Feb 1882	Belfast	Ireland 0 England 13
Steve Bloomer	5	16th Mar 1896	Cardiff	Wales 1 England 9
Willie Hall	5	16th Nov 1938	Manchester	England 7 Ireland 0
Malcolm Macdonald	5	16th April 1975	Wembley	England 5 Cyprus 0

— UNFASIONABLE CLUB XI —

If you turn out on Sunday mornings for the Dog and Duck in the local pub league you would assume, presumably correctly, that your chances of being selected to play for England were somewhat on the slim side. Yet playing for an obscure club was once no barrier to international recognition as this team of England players proves:

1. Harry Swepstone (**Pilgrims**, 6 caps, 1880–83)
2. Richard Baugh (**Stafford Road**, 2 caps, 1886–90)
3. W.S. Buchanan (**Clapham Rovers**, 1 cap, 1876)
4. Alfred Jones (**Great Lever**, 3 caps, 1882–83)
5. Gerald Dewhurst (**Liverpool Ramblers**, 1 cap, 1895)
6. John Edwards (**Shropshire Wanderers**, 1 cap, 1874)

7. A. Harvey (**Wednesbury Strollers**, 1 cap, 1881)
8. William Maynard (**1st Surrey Rifles**, 2 caps, 1872–76)
9. Albert Read (**Tufnell Park**, 1 cap, 1921)
10. Thomas Sorby (**Thursday Wanderers**, 1 cap, 1879)
11. George Tait (**Birmingham Excelsior**, 1 cap, 1881)

— ENGLAND'S OTHER TEAMS —

In addition to the senior side, England fields the following teams:

Team	Coach (as per 2006)
U21s	Peter Taylor
U20s	John Peacock
U19s	Martin Hunter
U18s	Brian Eastick
U17s	John Peacock
U16s	Kenny Swain
National Game XI (Non-league)	Paul Fairclough
Futsal Team (indoor football)	Graeme Dell
Women's senior team	Hope Powell
Women's U21s	Brent Hills
Women's U19s	Mo Marley
Women's U17s	Jane Ebbage

England also has no fewer than six different disabled teams: Blind, Partially Sighted, Deaf and Hearing Impaired, Cerebral Palsy, Learning Disabilities, Amputee.

— A NAZI BUSINESS —

One of the blackest moments in England's football history came on 14th May 1938 when, under pressure from the British ambassador to Germany to adhere to protocol, the team reluctantly agreed to give the Nazi salute before an international between Germany and England in the Olympic Stadium, Berlin.

"I've been in a shipwreck, a train crash, and inches short of a plane crash but the worst moment of my life was giving the Nazi salute in Berlin," said England captain Eddie Hapgood later. "I felt a fool heiling Hitler, but we went out determined to beat the Germans." In fact, Hitler was not present at the match, but some of his leading henchmen, including Goering, Goebbels, Hess and Ribbentrop were among the swastika-waving 110,000 crowd.

The German side, which included a number of Austrian players following their country's annexation by the Nazis earlier in the year, were fresh from 10 days' special training in the Black Forest. By contrast, the England side had not trained for the match and had just completed a gruelling domestic season. "We must have appeared a pretty washed-up bunch of athletes when we met the German team on the eve of the match," recalled Stanley Matthews. "They were as bronzed as Greek statues."

The super-fit Germans, though, were no match for a superb English side. 4–2 up at half-time, England eventually won 6–3 to expose the myth of Aryan supremacy. The irrepressible Matthews set up the best goal of the game, crossing for West Ham's Len Goulden to strike a ferocious 20-yard volley which ripped the net from the crossbar.

— CAPPED BOSSES —

The following England managers also played for their country:

Manager	Club(s)	Caps
Alf Ramsey	Southampton, Tottenham	32 (1949–53)
Joe Mercer	Everton	5 (1939)
Don Revie	Manchester City	6 (1954–56)
Bobby Robson	West Bromwich Albion	20 (1957–61)
Terry Venables	Chelsea	2 (1964)
Glenn Hoddle	Tottenham, Monaco	53 (1979–88)
Kevin Keegan	Liverpool, Hamburg, Southampton	63 (1973–82)
Peter Taylor	Crystal Palace	4 (1976)

— TAYLOR'S DUTCH DEBACLE —

Graham Taylor's unhappy reign as England manager was all but ended by a World Cup qualifying defeat away to Holland in October 1993. The result left England's hopes of reaching the finals in the USA hanging by the slimmest of threads, but it could have been a very different story.

"Napoleon wanted his generals to be lucky," Taylor observed when he left the England job. "I don't think he would have wanted me." And it's true that against Holland he, and England, were extraordinarily unlucky. For a start, Taylor was deprived of the services of the talismanic Paul Gascoigne, who was suspended. Or, as Gazza memorably put it: "Because of the booking I'll miss the Holland game. If selected."

In the match itself, fortune completely deserted England. Tony Dorigo and Paul Merson both hit the post with free-kicks, but the turning point of the game came around the hour mark. First, Holland captain Ronald Koeman hauled back David Platt just outside the penalty area with no other Dutch defender in sight. To Taylor's dismay, the German referee punished Koeman with a yellow card, rather than a red one. Two minutes later Koeman scored with a free-kick to give Holland the lead after the ref had ordered his first blocked effort to be retaken. Taylor was incandescent with rage, berating a FIFA official standing near the dug-out. "The referee has got me the sack," he fumed. "Thank him for that."

Sure enough, within a few weeks of England's 2–0 defeat in Rotterdam, Taylor was no longer England manager.

— '66 TOPS TV CHART —

England's epic encounter with West Germany in the 1966 World Cup final attracted the biggest ever TV audience in the UK, 32.3 million. The 1990 World Cup semi-final between the same countries also features in the all-time top 10 of British TV ratings successes:

Programme	Channel	Audience
1. England v West Germany, 1966 World Cup final	BBC1	32.3m
2. Funeral of Princess Diana, 1997	BBC1/ITV	32.1m
3. The Royal Family, 1969 documentary	BBC1/ITV	30.69m
4. EastEnders, Den and Angie divorce episode, 1986	BBC1	30.15m
5. Apollo 13 splashdown, 1970	BBC1/ITV	28.6m
6. Chelsea v Leeds, FA Cup final replay 1970	BBC1/ITV	28.49m
7. Charles and Di wedding ceremony, 1981	BBC1/ITV	28.4m
8. Princess Anne's wedding, 1973	BBC1/ITV	27.6m
9. Coronation Street, Blackpool tram death episode, 1989	ITV	26.93m
10. England v West Germany, 1990 World Cup	BBC1/ITV	26.2m

— QUICK OFF THE MARK —

The fastest recorded England goal was scored by Tommy Lawton after just 17 seconds of the friendly away to Portugal on 25th May 1947. The goal set England on their way to an impressive 10–0 victory.

Manchester United midfielder Bryan Robson scored England's fastest competitive goal when he struck after 27 seconds of the World Cup game against France in Bilbao, northern Spain, on 16th June 1982. Seven years later Robbo was at it again, this time striking England's quickest goal at Wembley after only 38 seconds against Yugoslavia on 13th December 1989.

However, Robson was made to look like a slowcoach by Teddy Sheringham, who scored just ten seconds after coming on as a substitute for England against Greece at Old Trafford on 6th October 2001.

Humiliatingly, the fastest goal conceded by England (and the fastest in World Cup history) was against minnows San Marino in Bologna on 17th November 1993 when winger Davide Gaultier took advantage of a poor back pass by Stuart Pearce to score after only 8.3 seconds, as described below to London radio listeners by Jonathan Pearce.

"Welcome to Bologna on Capital Gold, for England versus San Marino with Tennent's Pilsner Lager, brewed with Czechoslovakian yeast for that extra Pilsner taste and England are one down."

— TINSLEY ON TARGET —

Tinsley Lindley may sound like a camp London hairdresser but, in fact, he is England's most consistently prolific striker. Between 1886 and 1888 the Cambridge University forward scored in nine consecutive England matches to set a record which still stands today.

— HOME FROM HOMES —

Throughout their long history, England have played home games at 53 different venues around the country. No stadium, though, can rival the old Wembley record of hosting 223 England internationals between 1924 and 2000. The full list of England venues is as follows:

London
Kennington Oval, 10 games (1873–89)
Athletic Ground, Richmond, 1 game (1893)
Queen's Club, West Kensington, 1 game (1895)
Crystal Palace, 4 games (1897–1909)

Craven Cottage, 1 game (1907)
The Den, 1 game (1911)
Stamford Bridge, 3 games (1913–32)
Highbury, 11 games (1920–61)
Wembley, 223 games (1924–2000)
Selhurst Park, 1 game (1926)
White Hart Lane, 5 games (1933–2001)
Upton Park, 1 game (2003)

Blackburn
Alexander Meadows, 1 game (1881)
Leamington Road, 2 games (1885–87)
Ewood Park, 2 games (1891–1924)

Liverpool
Aigburth Park Cricket Club Ground, 1 game (1883)
Anfield, 7 games (1889–2002)
Goodison Park, 12 games (1895–1973)

Sheffield
Bramall Lane, 5 games (1883–1930)
Hillsborough, 2 games (1920–62)

Manchester
Whalley Range, 1 game (1885)
Old Trafford, 10 games (1926–2005)
Maine Road, 2 games (1946–49)
City of Manchester Stadium, 2 games (2004)

Crewe
Nantwich Road, 1 game (1888)

Stoke
The Victoria Ground, 3 games (1889–1936)

Sunderland
Newcastle Road, 1 game (1891)
Roker Park, 3 games (1899–1950)
Stadium of Light, 2 games (1999–2003)

Wolverhampton
Molineux, 4 games (1891–1956)

Birmingham
Wellington Road, Perry Barr, 1 game (1893)
Villa Park, 9 games (1899–2005)
The Hawthorns, 2 games (1922–24)

Derby
Derbyshire County Cricket Ground, 1 game (1895)
The Baseball Ground, 1 game (1911)
Pride Park, 1 game (2001)

Nottingham
Trent Bridge, 1 game (1897)
The City Ground, 1 game (1909)

Bristol
Ashton Gate, 2 games (1899–1913)

Southampton
The Dell, 1 game (1901)
St Mary's Stadium, 1 game (2002)

Newcastle
St. James' Park, 7 games (1901–2005)

Portsmouth
Fratton Park, 1 game (1903)

Middlesbrough
Ayresome Park, 3 games (1905–37)
The Riverside, 1 game (2003)

Bradford
Park Avenue, 1 game (1909)

Burnley
Turf Moor, 1 game (1927)

Blackpool
Bloomfield Road, 1 game (1932)

Huddersfield
Leeds Road, 1 game (1946)

Luton
Kenilworth Road, 1 game (1950)

Leeds
Elland Road, 2 games (1995–2002)

Leicester
Walker's Stadium, 1 game (2003)

Ipswich
Portman Road, 1 game (2003)

— ENGLAND AT THE WORLD CUP: 1970 —

Despite defending their trophy in the heat and humidity of Mexico, England were fancied by many observers to retain the World Cup. The team, though, were not popular with the locals, mainly because of Sir Alf Ramsey's disdainful attitude towards the Mexican press. It didn't help that striker Jeff Astle had to be carried off the plane somewhat the worse for wear when England arrived, an incident which, along with the Bobby Moore bracelet episode led to the team being condemned by local journalists as 'thieves and drunks'.

England's campaign began with a narrow win over Romania thanks to a single goal by 1966 hat-trick hero Geoff Hurst. Five days later, in hot and sticky conditions in Guadalajara, England gave eventual winners Brazil their toughest match of the competition. A tight first half provided an iconic moment when Gordon Banks somehow clawed away Pele's powerful downward header, but the England keeper was eventually beaten after the break by a close range shot from Jairzinho. For the final group game against Czechoslovakia, Sir Alf Ramsey felt sufficiently confident to make a number of changes and his makeshift side responded with a scrappy win that guaranteed England's progress to the knockout stage.

The quarter-final saw a rerun of the 1966 final as England were paired with West Germany. Two days before the match Banks went down with a stomach bug and, on the morning of the game, was declared unfit to play. He was replaced by Chelsea's Peter Bonetti, a relatively inexperienced international. For over an hour the enforced change appeared immaterial as England strolled into a 2–0 lead through Alan Mullery and Martin Peters. Then West Germany's Franz Beckenbauer gave his side hope with a low shot which slipped under Bonetti's dive. At this point Ramsey controversially substituted two of his best players, Bobby Charlton and Martin Peters, with the intention of saving them for the semi-final. However, the move backfired when, ten minutes from time, a back header by German striker Uwe Seeler looped over Bonetti and into the far corner for the equaliser. England were now wilting in the heat and as the match moved into extra-time the Germans took the initiative – and, eventually, the lead as Gerd 'Der Bomber' Muller volleyed in from six yards out. 11 minutes later, to howls of anguish which could be heard the length and breadth of the country, the referee blew time on England's four-year hold on the World Cup trophy.

Group table

	P	W	D	L	F	A	Pts
Brazil	3	3	0	0	8	3	6
England	3	2	0	1	2	1	4
Romania	3	1	0	2	4	5	2
Czechoslovakia	3	0	0	3	2	7	0

Date	Venue	Result
2nd June 1970	Guadalajara	England 1 Romania 0
7th June 1970	Guadalajara	England 0 Brazil 1
11th June 1970	Guadalajara	England 1 Czechoslovakia 0
14th June 1970	Leon (Q/F)	England 2 West Germany 3*

* After extra-time

England squad
Bobby Charlton (Manchester United, 4 apps), **Terry Cooper** (Leeds United, 4 apps), **Bobby Moore** (West Ham United, 4 apps), **Alan Mullery** (Tottenham, 4 apps), **Martin Peters** (Tottenham, 4 apps), **Alan Ball** (Everton, 3+1 apps), **Gordon Banks** (Stoke City, 3 apps), **Geoff Hurst** (West Ham United, 3 apps), **Brian Labone** (Everton, 3 apps), Francis Lee (Manchester City, 3 apps), **Keith Newton** (Everton, 3 apps), **Colin Bell** (Manchester City, 1+2 apps), **Jeff Astle** (WBA, 1+1 apps), **Tommy Wright** (Everton, 1+1 apps), **Peter Bonetti** (Chelsea, 1 app), **Jack Charlton** (Leeds United, 1 app), **Allan Clarke** (Leeds United, 1 app), **Peter Osgood** (Chelsea, 0+2 apps), **Norman Hunter** (Leeds United, 0+1 app), **Emlyn Hughes** (Liverpool, 0 apps), **Alex Stepney** (Manchester United, 0 apps), **Nobby Stiles** (Manchester United, 0 apps)

Goal scorers: Clarke 1, Hurst 1, Mullery 1, Peters 1

Tournament winners: Brazil

They said it

"At that moment I hated Gordon Banks more than any man in soccer. But when I cooled down I had to applaud him with my heart for the greatest save I had ever seen."

> Brazilian legend **Pele** on the save which denied him a goal in the England-Brazil match

"I felt sorry for Peter (Bonetti) but his role in our downfall was beyond argument. It was impossible not to wonder what would have happened had Gordon Banks played."

> **Geoff Hurst**, reflecting on England's World Cup exit

"Seeler's header was the goal that changed everything. It just hit the back of his head and went in, he never meant it."

Colin Bell, who came on for Bobby Charlton in the defeat against West Germany

— MATCH ABANDONED —

Two England games have been abandoned, although for very different reasons. On 17th May 1953 torrential rain caused the abandonment of England's fixture with Argentina in Buenos Aires after just 20 minutes. More than 40 years later, on 15th February 1995, England's match with the Republic of Ireland was called off after 27 minutes when crowd violence broke out at Lansdowne Road, Dublin. A minority of England fans, who were pictured on TV hurling seats at rival fans in the stand below them, were blamed for the disturbances.

— ANYONE FANCY GOING IN NETS? —

It wouldn't happen now but, on a number of occasions, England have had to put an outfield player in goal – and hope for the best! In the fourth ever England v Scotland game, at Kennington Oval on 6th March 1875, striker Alex Bonsar played the first 15 minutes in goal until the nominated keeper, Bill Carr of Owlerton FC, arrived. Bonsor managed to keep the Scots at bay during his unexpected turn in goal, but the England selectors were clearly unimpressed with Carr's time-keeping as he was never picked again.

On 22nd October 1927, inside-left Jack Ball of Bury, who was winning his first cap, volunteered to go in goal at half-time against Northern Ireland in Belfast when West Ham keeper Ted Hufton injured his wrist. Ball did well enough, conceding just one goal in England's 2–0 defeat but, having had little chance to impress in his normal position, was never called up by the selectors again. Two years previously, on 21st May 1925, Aston Villa's Billy Walker filled in as an emergency keeper after Millwall's Freddie Fox was injured during England's match away to France. Despite this disadvantage, England won the game 3–2.

— TREVOR'S CLEVER FINISH —

On 6th June 1981 England played a vital World Cup qualifier against Hungary in the Nepstadion, Budapest. The match, which England needed to win to keep alive their chances of qualifying for the finals in Spain the following year, is best remembered for a remarkable goal by midfielder Trevor Brooking. The England star's first time shot from the edge of the box was struck so perfectly that it flew past the Hungarian goalkeeper before wedging in the hoop holding up the corner of the net. "It was the best shot of my career," said Brooking later.

As the England players celebrated Brooking's superb effort, a group of disconsolate Hungarians formed in the six-yard box, wondering how to remove the ball from its unlikely perch. Brooking's wonder goal helped England to a 3–1 win and, just as importantly, became the benchmark by which all later 'screamers into the top corner' would be judged.

— CLUB AND COUNTRY —

On two occasions seven players from the same club have represented England in the same match. On 14th November 1934 seven Arsenal players (goalkeeper Frank Moss, George Male, Eddie Hapgood, Wilf Copping, Ray Bowden, Ted Drake and Cliff Bastin) played for England against Italy, appropriately enough at Highbury. The Gunners, or rather England, won the match against the then world champions 3–2 but the game was so bad-tempered and violent it was later dubbed 'The Battle of Highbury'.

Then, on 28th March 2001, Sven Goran-Eriksson fielded seven Manchester United players for England's World Cup qualifier against Albania. Five Reds started the match (Gary Neville, Nicky Butt, David Beckham, Paul Scholes and Andy Cole) and, by the final whistle, they had been joined by Old Trafford-based substitutes Wes Brown and Teddy Sheringham.

— ENGLAND DREAM TEAM —

In the summer of 2004 Channel 4 invited viewers to vote for their greatest ever England team. The eleven players selected showed a strong bias towards the 1966 World Cup winners and the most successful England players of a later generation, leaving no place for such stars of yesteryear as Stanley Matthews, Billy Wright or Jimmy Greaves.

Unsurprisingly, Sir Alf Ramsey was chosen as the manager of the team, which lined up as follows:

Gordon Banks
(73 caps, 1963–73)

George Cohen	**Tony Adams**	**Bobby Moore**	**Stuart Pearce**
(37 caps,	(66 caps,	(108 caps,	(78 caps,
1964–68)	(1987–2000)	1962–73)	1987–99)

David Beckham	**Paul Gascoigne**	**Bobby Charlton**	**Tom Finney**
(86 caps,	(57 caps,	(106 caps,	(76 caps,
1996–)	1988–98)	1958–70)	1947–58)

Alan Shearer   **Gary Lineker**
(63 caps, 1992–2000)   (80 caps, 1984–92)

— ENGLAND LEGENDS: SIR ALF RAMSEY —

The architect of England's 1966 World Cup triumph, Alf Ramsey had won 32 caps for his country in the previous decade. A neat, unflappable and hard-working right-back, Ramsey brought those same qualities to the job when he was appointed England manager in 1963 following Walter Winterbottom's resignation.

Against the odds, Ramsey had won the league title with unfashionable Ipswich Town, but many doubted whether he could enjoy similar success on the international stage. Ramsey, though, was supremely confident, telling the nation: "I think England will win the World Cup in 1966. We have the ability, strength, character and, perhaps above all, the players with the right temperament."

He was, of course, proved right as England lifted the Jules Rimet trophy following that epic final with West Germany at Wembley. Ramsey's contribution to the triumph was profound, no more so than in the area of tactics, where his 'wingless wonders' formation helped England to dominate the opposition in midfield. His motivational talk to his players before the start of extra-time in the final – "You've beaten them once, now go out there and bloody beat them again" – is also recognised by the players as a key moment in the historic victory.

Ramsey led England in their defence of the World Cup in 1970 but, following the quarter-final defeat by West Germany, his star began to dim. It didn't help that he was an introverted, reserved and taciturn figure whose relations with the press were often frosty. By the time of England's failure to qualify for the 1974 World Cup the knives were well and truly out for Ramsey and he was dismissed as national team manager in May 1974.

Sir Alf Ramsey Factfile

Born: Dagenham, 21st January 1920   **Died:** 28th April 1999
Clubs (player): Southampton, Tottenham
Caps: 32 (1949–53)
Goals: 3
England debut (player): Sweden 3 England 1, 13th May 1949
England debut (manager): France 5 England 2, 27th February 1963
International honours: England captain 3 times (1950–51), World Cup winner 1966

Others on Ramsey

"He was always very calm, even in moments of great crisis or celebration, and that rubbed off on the rest of us. It was reassuring and gave us confidence. He was not a screamer or ranter."
1966 World Cup winner **Martin Peters**

"We respected him because he showed us respect and our relationship with him was such that every player went out and gave his all for Alf."
England international **Jimmy Greaves**

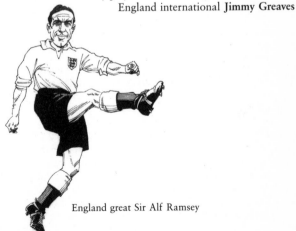

England great Sir Alf Ramsey

— GREAT EXCUSES —

"Seldom has an England side of high-class players been made to look so ordinary as this one was, and the only possible explanation is that our boys were sluggish from a too-sudden immersion in an ocean of food."

Daily Express reporter John MacAdam, suggesting that England's defeat in Switzerland in May 1947 was a result of over generous local hospitality

— THE MATCHES THAT COUNTED TWICE —

Home internationals were always significant dates in the England calendar but no more so than in seasons 1949/50 and 1953/54 when the championship doubled up as a qualifying group for the World Cup. With two teams qualifying each time, England were almost assured of filling one of the places – and that's how it turned out, too, as in both campaigns the Three Lions won all three of their games.

The idea of using the Home International Championship as a self-contained qualifying group was revived for the 1968 European Championships. This time the matches were spread over two seasons, 1966/67 and 1967/68, with only one country going through to a two-legged quarter-final. As world champions England were the favourites to win the group, but a surprise 3–2 home defeat by Scotland in April 1967 put qualification in doubt. Fortunately for Sir Alf Ramsey's men the Scots dropped points against Wales and Northern Ireland, allowing England to clinch a place in the last eight with a 1–1 draw in Glasgow in February 1968.

— DON REVIE'S FIRST ENGLAND TEAM —

Appointed England manager on 4th July 1974 former Leeds boss Don Revie had a reputation for favouring work rate, toughness and endeavour above skill, flair and creativity. Indeed, his win-at-all-costs football philosophy was perfectly illustrated when, after controversially resigning from the England job to take a lucrative coaching role in the United Arab Emirates, he said: "As soon as it dawned on me that we were short of players who combined skill and commitment, I should have forgotten all about trying to play more controlled, attractive football and settled for a real bastard of a team." Revie's first selection for a 3–0 win over Czechoslovakia at Wembley on 30th October 1974, though, contained some entertaining players along with notorious hardmen like Norman 'Bites Yer Legs' Hunter:

1. **Ray Clemence** (Liverpool)
2. **Paul Madeley** (Leeds United)
3. **Emlyn Hughes** (Liverpool, captain)
4. **Martin Dobson** (Burnley)
5. **Dave Watson** (Sunderland)
6. **Norman Hunter** (Leeds United)
7. **Colin Bell** (Manchester City)
8. **Gerry Francis** (QPR)
9. **Frank Worthington** (Leicester City)
10. **Mick Channon** (Southampton)
11. **Kevin Keegan** (Liverpool)
Substitutes: **Trevor Brooking** (West Ham United) and **Dave Thomas** (QPR)

— GET STRIPPED OFF, KEVIN —

With just four minutes to go of the infamous 1973 showdown with Poland at Wembley, England were in desperate need of a goal in their quest for World Cup qualification. Finally deciding to make a change, Sir Alf Ramsey called over to 'Kevin' to get stripped off. Substitute goalkeeper Ray Clemence immediately jumped to the task of helping Keegan strip off, yanked down his tracksuit trousers and accidentally pulled his shorts down too. It was the only glimpse of Keegan's 'magic' the crowd saw that night – Ramsey had been calling for Derby striker Kevin Hector!

— SCOTLAND, WORLD CHAMPIONS! —

The Unofficial Football World Championship (UFWC) is a novel way of calculating the best team in the world at any given moment, using a knock-out title system similar to the one used in boxing (**www.ufwc.com**). The winners of title matches become UFWC holders until they themselves are beaten and their crown passes to the victors. All very exciting, we're sure you'll agree, except very few fans or players are aware of the UFWC or which international fixtures are unofficial 'world title' clashes.

UFWC statisticians trace the origins of the title back to the very first international match between England and Scotland in 1872. That ended in a draw, but the following year England beat Scotland to become UFWC holders for the first time. Scotland took the title off their neighbours in 1874 and have since held it a record 85 times.

England are in second place, having held the title in 74 matches – the last time at Euro 2000 when an Alan Shearer header saw off reigning champions Germany. Sadly, Kevin Keegan's men threw away the UFWC title in their next match by losing to Romania.

Unofficial Football World Championship all-time rankings:

Country	Points
Scotland	85
England	**74**
Argentina	50
Russia	40
Holland	32

— CLASSIC CELEBRATIONS —

Gary Lineker, England 1 Republic of Ireland 1, 11th June 1990

Lineker's goal celebrations were usually low key, but after putting England ahead in this World Cup match in Cagliari, Italy, the deadly marksman slid on his bottom along the wet turf. It has been alleged that his celebration was designed to wipe his shorts on the wet turf after he had suffered an, ahem, embarrassing accident earlier in the game caused by a seafood meal eaten the previous day.

Paul Gascoigne, England 2 Scotland 0, 15th June 1996

After sealing England's victory in this Euro 96 derby clash with a superb individual strike, Gazza raced to the side of the goal and lay down with his mouth wide open. His delighted team-mates then took turns to squirt liquid from a sports drink into his mouth in a tongue-in-cheek reference to the 'dentist's chair' drinking episode which had generated negative headlines in the build up to the finals. Funny, clever and original, the celebration was almost as good as the goal.

Stuart Pearce, penalty shoot-out, England 0 Spain 0, 22nd June 1996

When Stuart Pearce stepped up to take a penalty in this Euro 96 shoot-out a hush descended on Wembley. Every fan knew that six years earlier Pearce had missed his kick in the World Cup penalty duel with West Germany, and had blamed himself for England's defeat. This time, though, Psycho drilled his spot-kick into the corner and raced towards the fans, fists clenched, eyes bulging and uncontrollably yelling a torrent of swearwords. Haunted by the events of 1990, Pearce had finally found 'closure'.

"Now lean back, sir, and have a gargle."

— LIFE DURING WARTIME —

England played no official matches during the World Wars but they did line up for a number of morale-boosting unofficial wartime internationals and, once the conflicts had ended, Victory Internationals. Here is a selection of results from those fixtures:

Date	Venue	Result
3rd May 1919	Glasgow	Scotland 3 England 4
11th October 1919	Cardiff	Wales 2 England 1
25th September 1943	Wembley	England 8 Wales 3
16th October 1943	Maine Road	England 8 Scotland 0
11th May 1946	Stamford Bridge	England 4 Switzerland 1

In the 1943 game against Wales the visitors were reduced to ten men when Welsh half-back Ivor Powell picked up an injury. Sportingly, England, who were leading 4–1, agreed to allow their reserve player Stan Mortensen to replace him. The Blackpool striker, who was uncapped by England at the time, went on to play 25 times for his country in official internationals.

— ENGLAND AT THE WORLD CUP: 1982 —

Following an unconvincing qualifying campaign in which they had seen their team lose to Romania, Switzerland and Norway, few fans held out much hope for England's World Cup prospects in Spain. The team, many agreed, were simply lucky to be there.

Yet, competing in the finals for the first time for 12 years, England got off to the best possible start in the opening game against France when Bryan Robson drilled home after just 27 seconds. England went on to win the match 3–1 and, after defeating both Czechoslovakia and Kuwait, topped their group with something to spare.

Rather than the usual knockout round, FIFA had decided that successful teams would play in a second round robin stage of four groups with the winners progressing to the semi-finals. England were given a tough draw, old adversaries West Germany and Spain making up the three-team group. After a dull 0–0 with the Germans, England needed to beat the hosts by two goals to reach the semi-finals but could only manage another goalless draw. Frustratingly, two excellent chances were spurned by substitutes Kevin Keegan and Trevor Brooking, both making their first appearances of the finals after missing the earlier part of the tournament through injury. So, somewhat bizarrely, Ron Greenwood's men returned home despite being undefeated and having conceded just one goal in five matches.

Group table

	P	W	D	L	F	A	Pts
England	3	3	0	0	6	1	6
France	3	1	1	1	6	5	3
Czechoslovakia	3	0	2	1	2	4	2
Kuwait	3	0	1	2	2	6	1

Second round group table

	P	W	D	L	F	A	Pts
West Germany	2	1	1	0	2	1	3
England	2	0	2	0	0	0	2
Spain	2	0	1	1	1	2	1

Date	Venue	Result
16th June 1982	Bilbao	England 3 France 1
20th June 1982	Bilbao	England 2 Czechoslovakia 0
25th June 1982	Bilbao	England 1 Kuwait 0
29th June 1982	Madrid	(2nd rd) England 0 West Germany 0
5th July 1982	Madrid	(2nd rd) Spain 0 England 0

England squad: Trevor Francis (Manchester City, 5 apps), **Paul Mariner** (Ipswich Town, 5 apps), **Mick Mills** (Ipswich Town, 5 apps), **Graham Rix** (Arsenal, 5 apps), **Peter Shilton** (Nottingham Forest, 5 apps), **Phil Thompson** (Liverpool, 5 apps), **Ray Wilkins** (Manchester United, 5 apps), **Terry Butcher** (Ipswich Town, 4 apps), **Steve Coppell** (Manchester United, 4 apps), **Bryan Robson** (Manchester United, 4 apps), **Kenny Sansom** (Arsenal, 4 apps), **Glenn Hoddle** (Tottenham, 1+1 apps), **Phil Neal** (Liverpool, 1+1 apps), **Tony Woodcock** (Arsenal, 1+1 apps), **Steve Foster** (Brighton, 1 app), **Trevor Brooking** (West Ham United, 0+1 apps), **Kevin Keegan** (Southampton, 0+1 apps), **Viv Anderson** (Nottingham Forest, 0 apps), **Ray Clemence** (Tottenham, 0 apps), **Joe Corrigan** (Manchester City, 0 apps), **Terry McDermott** (Liverpool, 0 apps), **Peter Withe** (Aston Villa, 0 apps)

Goal scorers: Francis 2, Robson 2 Mariner 1, Own goal 1

Tournament winners: Italy

They said it

"Bryan Robson's goal after 27 seconds was the best England goal I remember. Steve Coppell's long throw hit my head, dropping for Bryan to score. It was such a feeling, all the hard work prior felt worth it."

Terry Butcher on England's record start to
the competition against France

"I was definitely fit for the Spain game, and so was Trevor (Brooking). Leaving us on the bench was Ron Greenwood's biggest mistake."

Kevin Keegan

"I honestly thought we could have won the World Cup in 1982. We were strong in almost every department, and if we had been a little sharper in front of goal, who knows?"

Ron Greenwood

— BOBBY ROBSON'S FIRST ENGLAND TEAM —

Former Ipswich boss Bobby Robson took over the England team from Ron Greenwood in 1982 after the World Cup in Spain. His first team selection for a European Championship qualifier with Denmark was a controversial one, as there was no place for Greenwood's skipper Kevin Keegan. In Keegan's absence – which, it soon became apparent, was permanent – midfielder Ray Wilkins captained this side:

1. **Peter Shilton** (Southampton)
2. **Phil Neal** (Liverpool)
3. **Kenny Sansom** (Arsenal)
4. **Ray Wilkins** (Manchester United, captain)
5. **Russell Osman** (Ipswich Town)
6. **Terry Butcher** (Ipswich Town)
7. **Tony Morley** (Aston Villa)
8. **Bryan Robson** (Manchester United)
9. **Paul Mariner** (Ipswich Town)
10. **Trevor Francis** (Sampdoria)
11. **Graham Rix** (Arsenal)

— WORLD CUP FINAL 1966: THE PLAY —

In November 2004 a play entitled *World Cup Final 1966* opened at the Battersea Arts Centre in London. Written by Carl Heap and Tom Morris, the production attempted to recreate England's legendary triumph on stage, with an enthusiastic young cast and a variety of props including a set of mops. To add to the slightly surreal take on real-life events, two of the 1966 team (Martin Peters and Roger Hunt), were played by actresses. The play, which in 2005 moved on to Edinburgh, Manchester and Nottingham, received mixed reviews:

"Whereas previous shows at this address have had a wide family appeal, this one is limited to small boys – small boys, aged about 40, to whom the names Geoff Hurst, Martin Peters and Alan Ball mean something."

Lynn Gardener, *The Guardian*

"It's all splendidly enjoyable and more refreshing than a half-time orange – a clear winner."

Kevin Bourke, *Manchester Evening News*

"The 1966 campaign is neatly recreated with some good-natured national stereotyping and a great deal of prancing around with mops."

Dolan Cummings, www.culturewars.org.uk

— THE RUSSIAN LINESMAN —

Tofik Bakhramov was the linesman who signalled a goal in the 1966 World Cup final when Geoff Hurst's shot hit the underside of the West German crossbar and bounced down on, or as Bakhramov believed, over the line. After consulting with his silver-haired assistant, Swiss referee Gottfried Dienst pointed to the centre circle and England took a lead they were to maintain until the final whistle.

Although often described as 'the Russian linesman', Bakhramov was from Azerbaijan, now an independent country but a part of the Soviet Union in 1966. Originally a footballer, he took up refereeing after a serious leg injury ended his playing days. Bakhramov was elected on to the FIFA referee's panel in 1964 and later served as general secretary of the Football Federation of Azerbaijan, but it is for his role as a an eagle-eyed (or, from the German perspective, short-sighted) linesman later that he is most often remembered.

After his death in 1996 the Azeri national stadium in Baku was renamed the 'Tofik Bakhramov stadium'. In October 2004, shortly before England played a World Cup qualifier in Azerbaijan, a statue was erected to his memory in Baku. Among those attending the unveiling ceremony were FIFA President Sepp Blatter, former France captain Michel Platini and, fittingly, Geoff Hurst.

1966 World Cup final officials
Referee: Gottfried Dienst (Switzerland)
Linesmen: Tofik Bakhramov (USSR) and Karol Galba (Czechoslovakia)

— MAGICAL MAGYARS STUN ENGLAND —

England first hosted overseas opposition in 1923, beating Belguim 6–2 at Highbury. For the next 30 years they remained undefeated at home against non-UK sides, with the exception of a 2–0 reverse at the hands of the Republic of Ireland at Goodison Park in September 1949. The Eire side, though, was largely composed of players earning their living in the English leagues and so England's proud home record was still considered to be intact by the time Hungary visited Wembley on 25th November 1953.

The Hungarians were Olympic champions and on a magnificent run of 29 games without defeat. Players such as inside forward Ferenc Puskas, deep-lying centre-forward Nandor Hidegkuti and fellow striker Sandor Kocsis were key components in a wonderfully fluid team which frequently lived up to its nickname, the 'Magical Magyars'. Nor were the Hungarians relying on skill alone to beat England – rumour had it that their preparations included installing a fog-making machine on their training pitch to simulate London weather conditions. Even so, the expectation at Wembley was that the Hungarians would be sent packing; after all, England simply didn't lose at home.

The first indication, though, that the visitors might not crumble as easily as so many previous foreign teams came just before kick-off. "I remember that when I was called to the middle for the toss of the coin their captain Puskas was standing in the centre-circle all on his own juggling the match ball on his left foot," recalled England captain Billy Wright. "As I approached him he flicked the ball in the air, caught it on his thigh and then let it run down his shin and back on the centre spot. That was my first sight of Ferenc Puskas. He gave me a big grin as much as to say, 'Just wait until the rest of my tricks!'"

Within a minute of the match starting, Puskas split open the England defence with a superb pass which Hidegkuti lashed into the net from 20 yards. England soon equalised, but the Hungarians dominated the rest of the half, taking a 4–2 lead at the break. It finished 6–3, with Hidegkuti claiming a hat-trick and Puskas scoring twice. England's home record had been broken in the most shattering style, by a team playing swift, incisive, free-flowing football which left the hosts looking completely second-rate by comparison.

"Hungary were just a different class, and playing a style of football that was, well, foreign to us," acknowledged Wright years later. "It was a defeat that started a revolution in our game. We knew from that day on we needed to get into the modern world. They were playing a different game to us." Future England manager Alf Ramsey, however, was less impressed by the visitors, and years later would tell his players: "Four of those Hungarian goals came from outside our penalty area. We should never have lost."

In the long term, the lesson served up by the 'Magical Magyars' had a positive effect on English football as a new breed of coaches sought to improve the fitness, technical ability and tactical awareness of their players. In the short term, though, the Wembley thrashing had drastic repercussions for six members of the England team – including Ramsey, Stan Mortenson and centre-half Harry Johnston – none of whom played for their country again.

In many ways, the visit of the Hungarians marked a new passage in English football. Even that bastion of conservatism, *The Times*, appreciated that change was necessary if England was once again to be considered one of the game's leading nations. "English football can be proud of its past," its football correspondent opined. "But it must awake to a new future."

— 1966 LEGEND BOBBY TAKES ON ENGLAND —

Bobby Moore playing not for, but *against* England? It all sounds terribly unlikely, but in May 1976 the former Three Lions skipper lined up against his old team-mates when he captained an American side in the USA Bicentennial Cup.

The tournament included four teams, England, Brazil, Italy and Team America, whose multi-national squad was drawn from players performing in the North American Soccer League. Moore, who was playing a summer season for San Antonio Thunder, led out a scratch team in Philadelphia which included fellow former England international Tommy Smith, Welsh centre-half Mike England and onetime Italian international Giorgio Chinaglia. George Best and Rodney Marsh were also originally selected for the Team America squad, but dropped out when they were not guaranteed starts in all three games.

England won the match, which was not recognised by the Football Association as an official international, by three goals to one.

— 1966 WORLD CUP FINAL: THE STATS —

	England	Germany
Goals	4	2
Shots on target	23	25
Corners	6	12
Fouls	22	16

— OVERCAPPED? V UNDERCAPPED? —

If the two England teams listed below played a match which of them, do you think, would win? A tough call, but the difference is the first team won a mountain of caps between them, while the second lot hardly won enough to open a second-hand hat stall in Peckham market . . .

Overcapped?
1. **David James** (32 caps, 1997–2005)
2. **Phil Neville** (52 caps, 1996–2005)
3. **Wayne Bridge** (21 caps, 2002–)
4. **Carlton Palmer** (18 caps, 1992–93)
5. **Terry Fenwick** (20 caps, 1984–88)
6. **Martin Keown** (43 caps, 1992–2002)
7. **Kieron Dyer** (28 caps, 1999–2005)
8. **David Batty** (42 caps, 1991–99)

9. **Luther Blissett** (14 caps, 1982–84)
10. **Emile Heskey** (43 caps, 1999–2004)
11. **Owen Hargreaves** (29 caps, 2001–)

Undercapped?
1. **Alex Stepney** (1 cap, 1968)
2. **Rob Jones** (8 caps, 1992–95)
3. **Paul Reaney** (3 caps, 1968–71)
4. **Terry Venables** (2 caps, 1964)
5. **Kevin Beattie** (9 caps, 1975–77)
6. **Steve Perryman** (1 cap, 1982)
7. **Stan Bowles** (5 caps, 1974–77)
8. **Alan Hudson** (2 caps, 1975)
9. **Peter Osgood** (4 caps, 1970–73)
10. **Matt Le Tissier** (8 caps, 1994–97)
11. **Rodney Marsh** (9 caps, 1971–73)

— WORLD CUP BOYCOTT —

The World Cup is such a major event these days it seems incredible that England didn't even bother to enter the first three tournaments in the 1930s.

The Three Lions' boycott of the competition stemmed from a long-running dispute with FIFA about the definition of amateurism. In 1928 FIFA insisted that amateur footballers competing at the Olympic games should be paid 'broken time payments' to make up for their lost earnings. The four British Football Associations objected to the payments, believing that a strict distinction between amateurs and professionals needed to be preserved.

As a protest against the policy, the four home countries pulled out not only of the Olympics but FIFA too. The result was that teams from the UK did not participate in the World Cups of 1930, 1934 or 1938. The rift was healed in 1946 when the British associations rejoined FIFA, although the issue of 'broken time payments' remained a contentious one until the distinction between amateurs and professionals was finally dropped in 1974.

— LET THERE BE LIGHT —

England first played under floodlights against the USA at Yankee Stadium, New York on 8th June 1953. Playing under lights clearly agreed with Walter Winterbottom's team who gained some revenge for their humiliating defeat against the same opposition at the 1950 World Cup by winning 6–3.

Two years later, on 30th November 1955, England played under floodlights for the first time at Wembley in a 4–1 victory against Spain.

— 1966 AND ALL THAT —

The 10 greatest victories in England's history . . .

No.	Date	Venue	Result
1	30th July 1966	Wembley	England 4 West Germany 2*
2	1st Sept 2001	Munich	Germany 1 England 5
3	16th May 1948	Turin	Italy 0 England 4
4	10th June 1984	Rio de Janeiro	Brazil 0 England 2
5	26th July 1966	Wembley	England 2 Portugal 1
6	15th April 1961	Wembley	England 9 Scotland 3
7	18th June 1996	Wembley	England 4 Holland 1
8	23rd July 1966	Wembley	England 1 Argentina 0
9	24th May 1975	Wembley	England 5 Scotland 1
10	7th June 2002	Sapporo	England 1 Argentina 0

* After extra-time

— ENGLAND AT THE WORLD CUP: 1986 —

England's bid to win the 1986 World Cup in Mexico got off to an appalling start when, after defeat to Portugal and a draw with Morocco, the team's hopes of progressing to the knockout stage were hanging by the slimmest of threads. Even worse, manager Bobby Robson had lost two of his key performers, injured skipper Bryan Robson and midfielder Ray Wilkins, suspended after becoming the first England player to be sent off at the finals.

Fortunately, the new-look team Robson fielded in the must-win final group game against Poland gelled instantly, striker Gary Lineker scoring all three goals in a convincing 3–0 win. Another vibrant display, and two more Lineker goals, saw off Paraguay in the last 16, setting up a dramatic quarter-final encounter with Argentina.

After a cagey first half, the match in Mexico City exploded into life shortly after the break when Argentina's captain and star player, Diego Maradona, clearly used his hand to flick the ball the ball into the net. Despite furious protests from the England players the goal stood. Minutes later, Maradona showed why he was acclaimed as one of the greatest players ever, dribbling past the entire England defence before planting the ball past goalkeeper Peter Shilton. A late headed goal by Golden Boot winner Lineker was not enough to save England, who returned home feeling both cheated and outclassed by the same man, World Cup winner Diego Maradona.

Group table

	P	W	D	L	F	A	Pts
Morocco	3	1	2	0	3	1	4
England	3	1	1	1	3	1	3
Poland	3	1	1	1	1	3	3
Portugal	3	1	0	2	2	4	2

Date	Venue	Result
3rd June 1986	Monterrey	England 0 Portugal 1
6th June 1986	Monterrey	England 0 Morocco 0
11th June 1986	Monterrey	England 3 Poland 0
18th June 1986	Mexico City (Last 16)	England 3 Paraguay 0
22nd June 1986	Mexico City (Q/F)	England 1 Argentina 2

England squad: Terry Butcher (Ipswich, 5 apps) **Gary Lineker** (Everton, 5 apps), **Glenn Hoddle** (Tottenham, 5 apps), **Kenny Sansom** (Arsenal, 5 apps), **Peter Shilton** (Southampton, 5 apps), **Gary Stevens** (Everton, 5 apps), **Terry Fenwick** (QPR, 4 apps), **Steve Hodge** (Aston Villa, 3+2 apps), **Peter Beardsley** (Newcastle, 3+1 apps), **Peter Reid** (Everton, 3 apps), **Trevor Steven** (Everton, 3 apps), **Mark Hateley** (AC Milan, 2+1 apps), **Chris Waddle** (Tottenham, 2+1 apps), **Bryan Robson** (Manchester United, 2 apps), **Ray Wilkins** (AC Milan, 2 apps), **Alvin Martin** (West Ham United, 1 app), **Gary Stephens** (Tottenham, 0+2 apps), **John Barnes** (Watford, 0+1 apps), **Kerry Dixon** (Chelsea, 0+1 apps), **Viv Anderson** (Arsenal, 0 apps), **Gary Bailey** (Manchester United, 0 apps), **Chris Woods** (Norwich City, 0 apps)

Goal scorers: Lineker 6, Beardsley 1

Tournament winners: Argentina

They said it

"No one came to terms with the heat of Monterrey. Dr Vernon Edwards stuck the thermometer in the pitch and said 'guess the temperature'. '90?' 'It's 104?' 'For God's sake don't tell the players,' I said, 'they'll melt thinking about it!'"

Bobby Robson

"A little bit the hand of God, a little bit the head of Diego."

Argentina captain **Diego Maradona,** describing his
first goal against England

"It wasn't the hand of God. It was the hand of a rascal. God had nothing to do with it."

Bobby Robson rules out divine intervention in Maradona's goal

— QUICKFIRE HAT-TRICK —

The fastest England hat-trick was scored by Willie Hall against Northern Ireland at Old Trafford on 16th November 1938. The Tottenham forward hit three goals in just three and a half minutes late in the first half to set a record which is unlikely ever to be beaten. For good measure, Hall grabbed another two goals as England trounced the Irish 7–0. This is how *The Times* reported Hall's extraordinary feat:

> *"England looked the better side, but there was little to suggest that three goals would be so quickly scored and that the match would be so soon virtually over. The first of Hall's goals seemed unnecessary. Matthews put over a centre which looked innocent enough, but the Irish defence faltered and Hall was able to shoot thorough. Almost immediately after the kick-off Hall scored again, this time from the inside-left position. His shot went low into the corner of the net, and immediately afterwards came another goal. The ball came from the left, Twoomey came out, and before he was properly back and on his balance Hall had taken his third chance."*

— ENGLAND LEGENDS: GARY LINEKER —

Despite not making his international debut until he was almost 24, Gary Lineker is the second highest scorer in England history with 48 goals. A natural finisher, Lineker came alive in the penalty area where his ability to snaffle half chances was reminiscent of another Spurs legend and poacher supreme, Jimmy Greaves.

The Leicester-born striker's international reputation was forged in the heat of Mexico, when his six goals at the 1986 World Cup earned him the tournament's Golden Boot. Lineker's hat-trick against Poland in a vital group game victory perfectly illustrated his striking style, all three goals being fired home from close range with a single touch of the ball. Speed of thought, along with speed of movement, were the key factors in enabling Lineker to react before his marker each time.

Recovering from a bout of hepatitis, Lineker was subdued during England's disappointing 1988 European Championship campaign, but he was back to his best at the 1990 World Cup. Another four goals, which included two nerveless penalties against Cameroon and a typically composed finish against West Germany in the semi-final, established him as England's most prolific World Cup scorer ever.

Appointed captain by Graham Taylor in 1990, Lineker's relationship with his manager deteriorated when he was publicly criticised after a poor display against Brazil in May 1992. In the same match Lineker missed a penalty, and the opportunity to equal Bobby Charlton's longstanding England goalscoring record. Lineker's international career ended unhappily as he was controversially substituted by Taylor in his final England match, the European Championship defeat by Sweden in June 1992.

Gary Lineker Factfile
Born: Leicester, 30th November 1960
Clubs: Leicester City, Everton, Barcelona, Tottenham
Caps: 80 (1984–92)
Goals: 48
England debut: Scotland 1 England 1, 26th May 1984 (sub)
International honours: England captain 18 times (1990–92), Golden Boot (1986 World Cup)

Others on Lineker

"Lineker was a goalscorer to his bones. His domain was the penalty area. Gary was a one-touch finisher, quite adept in the air for his height, perceptive in his positioning, good on the turn and exemplary in the six-yard box."

Sir Bobby Robson

"He could make the most penetrating runs I ever saw and if you delivered the ball properly he was almost certain to get you a goal. There was a cleverness, a cuteness, to Lineker's runs that I don't think anyone else has demonstrated for England."

England team-mate **Tony Adams**

Demon goal poacher Gary Lineker

— CHANGE OF DIRECTION —

A selection of unlikely new careers for former England internationals once they'd hung up their boots:

Mick Channon (46 caps, 1972–77) Racehorse trainer
Tony Dorigo (15 caps, 1989–93) Lifestyle manager
Jimmy Greaves (57 caps, 1959–67) Carpet salesman
Francis Lee (27 caps, 1968–72) Toilet roll entrepreneur
Maurice Norman (23 caps, 1962–64) Petrol pump attendant
Neil Webb (26 caps, 1987–92) Postman
Ray Wilson (63 caps, 1960–68) Undertaker
Billy Wright (105 caps, 1946–59) Television executive

— DERBY DAYS —

England have played far more games against Scotland, Wales and Northern Ireland (formerly Ireland) than any other countries in the world. The Three Lions' overall record against the other three UK teams reads as follows

	P	W	D	L	F	A
Scotland	110	45	24	41	192	169
Wales	99	64	21	14	242	90
Northern Ireland	98	75	16	7	323	81

— ENGLAND SCANDAL SITES —

Lancaster Gate Hotel, London

Before flying out to play Portugal in a friendly in May 1964, the England team stayed at this hotel in west London. Unenthused by the prospect of spending another night in playing cards, a group of players, including Bobby Moore, Bobby Charlton, Gordon Banks and Jimmy Greaves popped out for a night on the town. When they returned to their hotel rooms at around midnight they found their passports lying on their beds, a coded message from manager Alf Ramsey that their escapade did not meet with his approval. Ramsey later told the players involved that they would have been sent home if replacements had been available.

Fuego Verde jewellery store, Bogota

In May 1970 England captain Bobby Moore was accused of stealing an emerald bracelet worth £625 from a jewellery store in the lobby of the El Tequendama hotel in Bogota, Colombia, where England were playing a warm up match before the start of the World Cup in Mexico. When the England team returned to Bogota from another friendly match in Ecuador, Moore was arrested and detained at the house of a Colombian FA official while the rest of the squad flew on to Mexico. After three days Moore was released and the charges against him were eventually dropped.

China Jump Club, Hong Kong

After playing a warm up match in Hong Kong ahead of Euro 96, the England players were given a night off and headed to a trendy nightclub to celebrate Paul Gascoigne's 29th birthday. The club's unique feature was a dentist's chair which customers would recline in while bar staff poured a mixture of intoxicating spirits into their gaping mouths. Some of the players found this gimmick impossible to resist, with predictable results. The English media were appalled by the players' boozy antics on the eve of an important tournament and the incident was the subject of negative headlines for some days after.

Cathay Pacific flight, Hong Kong to London
Following the 'dentist's chair' incident, the England squad returned home from Hong Kong on a Cathay Pacific flight. During the 13-hour journey a number of state-of-the-art TV sets and an overhead locker were damaged in the upper business class section, allegedly by members of the England team. At the time, the players adopted a policy of 'collective responsibility' for the damage and were each docked £5,000 to pay for the repairs; some years later, however, Paul Gascoigne admitted in his autobiography that he had punched and broken two of the TV sets.

La Manga sports complex, Spain
Shortly before the start of 1998 World Cup in France the England squad spent some time training at the La Manga complex in southern Spain. At the end of the stay manager Glenn Hoddle had to announce his trimmed down squad for the tournament, and arranged to tell each player individually whether or not they would be going to the World Cup. One of the players Hoddle left out of his final squad was Paul Gascoigne. According to Hoddle, Gazza reacted violently to the bad news, smashing his fist into a large lamp and swearing "like a man possessed". The midfielder never played for England again.

Burnham Beeches Hotel, Bucks
After England had beaten Scotland at Hampden Park in the first leg play-off qualifier for Euro 2000 the squad returned to their team hotel in readiness for the second leg at Wembley. While some of the London-based players were allowed home by England manager Kevin Keegan, the rest stayed up late with their boss, drinking, playing cards and watching a boxing match on TV. The press soon got hold of the story, many reporters arguing that a late-night drinking session was hardly the best preparation for an important international in four days' time. The fact that England played poorly and lost the return game suggested they may well have been right.

— PICKLES SAVES THE DAY —

On March 20th 1966 the World Cup trophy was stolen from a glass-fronted cabinet in Central Hall, Westminster where it was on show prior to that year's tournament in England. The police launched a huge operation to recover the trophy and eventually arrested 47-year-old Edward Betchley in connection with the theft.

The Cup was still missing, however, and wasn't found until Pickles, a black-and-white mongrel dog, discovered it under a bush while out for a walk on Beulah Hill, south London, with his owner Dave Corbett. "I saw him sniffing a bundle so I tore off the paper and realised my dog had found the World Cup," recalled Corbett.

Pickles became an instant national hero and was rewarded with a year's supply of his favourite nibbles by a dog food company. Sadly, later the same year, he was strangled by his lead while chasing after a cat.

— ONE-OFF OPPONENTS —

While England have played the likes of Germany, Italy and Scotland dozens of times, their meetings with some of world football's more obscure nations have been less frequent. Here's a list of opponents England have locked swords with just the once:

Date	Venue	Result
13th June 1908	Prague	Bohemia 0 England 4
24th May 1970	Quito	Ecuador 0 England 2
25th June 1982	Bilbao	England 1 Kuwait 0
24th May 1986	Vancouver	Canada 0 England 1
12th June 1991	Kuala Lumpar	Malaysia 2 England 4
29th April 1992	Moscow	CIS 2 England 2
23rd May 1996	Beijing	China 0 England 3
18th Nov 1998	Wembley	England 2 Czech Republic 0
21st May 2002	Seoguipo	South Korea 1 England 1
3rd June 2003	Leicester	England 2 Serbia-Montenegro 1

— COLE'S CONFUSION —

Spare a thought for Andy Cole (or Andrew Cole, as we must now call him). The first four times the then Manchester United striker was picked to play for his country he did so under a different England manager. Little wonder, perhaps, that the prolific Premiership marksman failed to produce his club form at international level.

These are the quartet of games where Coley had to introduce himself to the man in charge – "Hello, I'm Andy, I mean Andrew Cole . . ." – before running out in the famous white shirt:

Cole cap no.	Date	England manager	Match result
1	29th March 1995	Terry Venables	England 0 Uruguay 0
2	12th Feb 1997	Glenn Hoddle	England 0 Italy 1
3	10th Feb 1999	Howard Wilkinson*	England 0 France 2
4	27th March 1999	Kevin Keegan	England 3 Poland 1

* Caretaker-manager

On a similar note, goalkeeper David Seaman played for England under no fewer than seven managers: Bobby Robson, Graham Taylor, Terry Venables, Glenn Hoddle, caretaker Howard Wilkinson, Kevin Keegan and Sven-Goran Eriksson. It would have been eight, but caretaker Peter Taylor didn't select Seaman for the friendly against Italy in Turin in November 2000.

— LET'S GO GOAL CRAZY! —

England's biggest win came way back in 1882 when Ireland were thrashed 13–0 in Belfast. 17 years later England again racked up a baker's dozen against the same opponents, but at least the Irish managed a couple of consolation goals on that occasion.

Overall, England have hit double figures five times:

Date	Venue	Result
2nd Feb 1882	Belfast	Ireland 0 England 13
18th Feb 1899	Sunderland	England 13 Ireland 2
8th June 1908	Vienna	Austria 1 England 11
25th May 1947	Lisbon	Portugal 0 England 10
27th May 1964	New York	USA 0 England 10

— ENGLAND AT THE WORLD CUP: 1990 —

Drawn in a tough group, England began with an uninspiring 1–1 draw against bogey side Ireland in rain-sodden Sardinia. A better performance against Holland followed, but England again only managed a point. Once more, everything depended on the final group game against Egypt, which was decided in England's favour by Mark Wright's header.

Under pressure from his more experienced players, England manager Bobby Robson had switched to a sweeper system against Holland and he retained the formation for the last 16 meeting with Belgium. A tight game looked to be heading for penalties until midfielder Paul Gascoigne's free-kick was superbly volleyed in by David Platt for the winning goal. Gascoigne was again outstanding in a bruising quarter-final with surprise packages Cameroon, which was again won in extra-time by the second of two Gary Lineker penalties.

In the semi-final against West Germany in Turin England fell behind to a cruelly deflected shot in the second half, but showing admirable spirit and no little skill equalised through a well-taken Lineker goal with ten minutes left. Yet again, the match went into extra-time but no goals were forthcoming, only a booking for a distraught Gascoigne, which meant he would miss the final should England get there. On to penalties, then, and to the dismay of 30 million fans watching back home, Stuart Pearce and Chris Waddle were unable to match the clinical efficiency of the Germans, who went on to beat Argentina in the final.

Group table

	P	W	D	L	F	A	Pts
England	3	1	2	0	2	1	4
Rep. Ireland	3	0	3	0	2	2	3
Holland	3	0	3	0	2	2	3
Egypt	3	0	2	1	1	2	2

Date	Venue	Result
11th June 1990	Cagliari	England 1 Rep. Ireland 1
16th June 1990	Cagliari	England 0 Holland 0
21st June 1990	Cagliari	England 1 Egypt 0
27th June 1990	Bologna (Last 16)	England 1 Belgium 0*
1st July 1990	Naples (Q/F)	England 3 Cameroon 2*
4th July 1990	Turin (S/F)	England 1 West Germany 1*^
7th July 1990	Bari (3rd/4th place)	Italy 2 England 1

* After extra-time

^ West Germany won 4–3 on penalties

England squad: Gary Lineker (Tottenham, 7 apps), **Peter Shilton** (Derby County, 7 apps), **Des Walker** (Nottingham Forest, 7 apps), **Chris Waddle** (Marseille, 6+1 apps), **Paul Gascoigne** (Tottenham, 6 apps), **Paul Parker** (QPR, 6 apps), **Stuart Pearce** (Nottingham Forest, 6 apps), **Mark Wright** (Derby County, 6 apps), **Terry Butcher** (Rangers, 5 apps), **John Barnes** (Liverpool, 5 apps), **David Platt** (Aston Villa, 3+3 apps), **Peter Beardsley** (Liverpool, 3+2 apps), **Steve McMahon** (Liverpool, 3+1 apps), **Bryan Robson** (Manchester United, 2 apps), **Gary Stevens** (Rangers, 2 apps), **Steve Bull** (Wolves, 1+2 apps), **Trevor Steven** (Rangers, 1+2 apps), **Tony Dorigo** (Chelsea, 1 app), **Neil Webb** (Manchester United, 0+1 apps), **Steve Hodge** (Nottingham Forest, 0 apps), **David Seaman** (QPR, 0 apps)*, **Chris Woods** (Rangers, 0 apps)
* Replaced after the start of the tournament by **Dave Beasant** (Chelsea, 0 apps)

Goal scorers: Lineker 4, Platt 3, Wright 1

Tournament winners: West Germany

They said it

"Neil Webb threw me a towel because I was sobbing my heart out. I had it over my head like a convicted criminal leaving a court house."
Stuart Pearce, recalling his reaction to missing in the England-West Germany penalty shoot-out

"In training, they knocked them in like cherries."
Bobby Robson on England's penalty-taking practice

"No team deserved to win, because no team deserved to lose."
German coach **Franz Beckenbauer** to Bobby Robson after the semi-final

— A CHANGE OF TACK —

The England team of the 1870s were largely a side of dribblers, but despite their crowd-pleasing skills they only rarely beat the Scots, who were quicker to appreciate the benefits of a game based around passing the ball.

England's early defeats provoked irritation among the public, an indication of the passions international football would arouse in the years to come. After one particularly heavy defeat, a 7–2 thrashing at the hands of the Scots in Glasgow in 1878, a debate began about the playing style of the England team.

Shortly after the game, *Bell's Life* published a letter, signed by 'A Disgusted Englishman', which read:

> *"The England players we had down this time were a splendid lot of players individually, but to my idea they played very selfishly, each one of them appearing to play for himself and not for the success of the side."*

England's fortunes began to turn around after a group of ex-Varsity men formed the Corinthians club in 1882 with the idea of drawing all the best amateur players together. This provided England with a group of players who had built up an understanding at club level, Corinthian players forming the basis of the team along with a smattering of professionals from the north and midlands. Thanks to the influence of the Corinthians the value of team play came to be recognised by England's players. As one Scottish player, Walter Arnott, put it: "The Corinthians, who have perfected the tactics of three inside forwards, have created as good and effective a style as I have seen."

England, though, did not gain dominance over the Scots until the late 1880s when professionalism, which was legalised in England in 1885, prompted a mass exodus of Scottish players from north of the border. The Scottish authorities' reaction was to ban these players from representing their country, a measure which provided England with a huge advantage until the restriction was lifted in 1896. Indeed, England didn't lose to the Scots during the 1890s until that year, a 2–1 defeat in Glasgow.

— YOU'LL NEVER BEAT THE ENGLAND! —

England are unbeaten against 38 FIFA-registered countries – a stat which sounds rather impressive, particularly if you don't take into account the fact that we've only played the likes of China, Ecuador and South Korea once each. However, England do have some genuinely striking undefeated records against a number of countries:

Opponent	P	W	D	L	F	A
Finland	11	9	2	0	36	7
Turkey	10	8	2	0	31	0
Luxembourg	9	9	0	0	47	3
Greece	8	6	2	0	19	3

— OFF THE BENCH —

The International Football Association Board first permitted substitutes in international friendlies in 1932. The idea took a while to catch on, however, and it wasn't until 18th May 1950 that England used their first ever substitute, Wolves winger Jimmy Mullen replacing Newcastle's Jackie Milburn after ten minutes in a 4–1 win over Belgium in Brussels. Mullen quickly proved the value of fresh legs by scoring one of England's goals.

Substitutes were first allowed in competitive matches at the 1970 World Cup in Mexico. England manager Sir Alf Ramsey took advantage of the new rule by bringing on two subs – Everton's Tommy Wright and Chelsea's Peter Osgood – in his team's first match of the tournament against Romania in Guadalajara on 2nd June 1970. Later in the same tournament, against West Germany in the quarter-finals, Ramsey controversially substituted Bobby Charlton and Martin Peters for Colin Bell and Norman Hunter. At the time of the changes England were leading 2–1 but went on to lose the match in extra-time.

It wasn't until 27th June 1990 that an England player came off the bench to score in the World Cup, sub David Platt hitting a last-minute winner against Belgium in Bologna. Since then, the only England sub to score at the World Cup finals is Michael Owen, who found the net against Romania in Toulouse on 22nd June 1998.

— POSH BOYS XI —

"What a jolly jape, I'm off to play footer for England – toodle pip!" Not a sentence you'd expect to hear these days in the corridors of Eton or Harrow, or the cloisters of Oxford or Cambridge, but go back to the late nineteenth century and the England team was packed with players from the country's top public schools and universities.

1. Morton Betts (**Old Harrovians**, 1 cap, 1877)
2. Robert Topham (**Casuals**, 2 caps, 1893–94)
3. Samuel Day (**Old Malvernians**, 3 caps, 1906)
4. William Wickworth (**Old Westminsters**, 2 caps, 1892–93)
5. George Cotterill (**Old Brightonians**, 4 caps, 1891–93)
6. Edward Parry (**Old Carthusians**, 3 caps, 1879–82)
7. Percy Fairclough (**Old Foresters**, 1 cap, 1878)
8. Alfred Lyttleton (**Cambridge University**, 1 cap, 1877)
9. Cuthbert Ottoway (**Oxford University**, 2 caps, 1872–74)
10. Edward Johnson (**Saltley College**, 2 caps, 1880–84)
11. Herbert Whitfield (**Old Etonians**, 1 cap, 1879)

— THE FIRST HAT-TRICK —

The first players to score hat-tricks for England were the Aston Villa duo Howard Vaughton and Arthur Brown. The pair battled for the match ball after England's 13–0 thrashing of Ireland in Belfast in 1882, the first ever meeting between the two countries. By rights, Vaughton had a better claim on the ball as he scored five goals, while Brown only managed four. In the years since, Ireland (from 1923, Northern Ireland) became the favoured opposition of goal-hungry English strikers with a record 20 hat-tricks being scored against our near neighbours.

— THE BATTLE OF HIGHBURY —

The meeting of England and Italy, reigning world champions, at Highbury on 14th November 1934 was a major event in both countries. Advance publicity for the game described it as, "the most important football match that has been played anywhere in the world since the Great War," and victory in the contest was considered a matter of national pride in both England and Mussolini's Italy.

Nor were the Italian players merely playing for pride. Victory over England was considered a huge scalp, so much so that the Italians were each promised £150, an Alfa Romeo car and exemption from military service should they triumph. Unsurprisingly, given these goodies on offer, they were very keen to win.

The violence that the game is now remembered for was sparked after just three minutes when Italy's star player, the Argentinian-born centre-half Luisito Monti, had to be taken to hospital in agony following an injury to his foot. The Italians were convinced that Monti had been deliberately targeted, and responded with a series of vicious challenges.

England captain Eddie Hapgood also had to go off after suffering a broken nose, and said later: "It was difficult to play like a gentleman when somebody closely resembling an enthusiastic member of the Mafia is wiping his studs down your legs."

Between the stoppages for fouls and treatment of injuries, England swept into a 3–0 lead before being hauled back to 3–2 in the second half. The result, though, was overshadowed by the Italians' violent play which led some members of the FA to question whether England should continue to play international football. One FA councillor summed up the post-match mood after 'The Battle of Highbury' when he said: "It is quite impossible, if we are to conserve all that is good in the game, that we should continue to play matches against the players of nations, who either because of temperament or lack of knowledge of the rules, are unable to distinguish between that which is right and that which is wrong."

ENGLAND KITS 1958-2006

www.classickits.co.uk

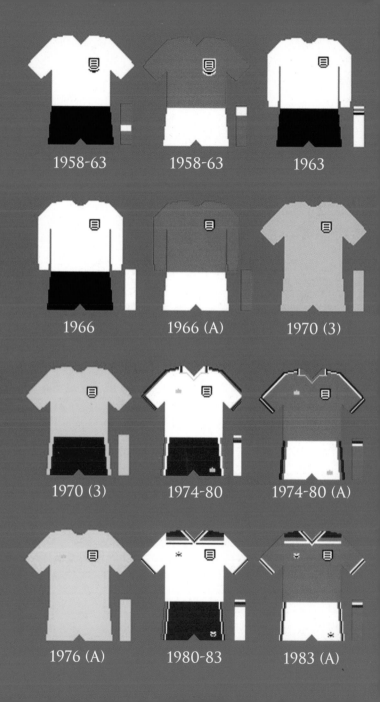

1958-63   1958-63   1963

1966   1966 (A)   1970 (3)

1970 (3)   1974-80   1974-80 (A)

1976 (A)   1980-83   1983 (A)

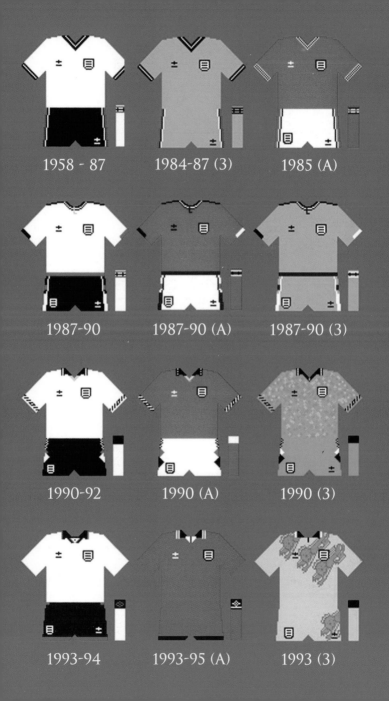

1958 - 87

1984-87 (3)

1985 (A)

1987-90

1987-90 (A)

1987-90 (3)

1990-92

1990 (A)

1990 (3)

1993-94

1993-95 (A)

1993 (3)

1995-96

1996 (A)

1997 - 98

1997-00 (A)

1999-2001

2000-02 (A)

2001-03

2002-04 (A)

2003-05

2004 (A)

2005-07

2006-08 (A)

— NAME THAT CLUB —

A selection of England internationals whose names are also Football League clubs:

Frederick **Blackburn** (3 caps, 1901–04)
George **Blackburn** (1 cap, 1924)
Geoff **Bradford** (1 cap, 1955)
Lindsay **Bury** (2 caps, 1877–79)
Bobby **Charlton** (106 caps, 1958–70)
Jack **Charlton** (35 caps, 1965–70)
Robert Frederick **Chelsea** Moore (108 caps, 1962–73)
Alan **Sunderland** (1 cap, 1980)
Richard **York** (2 caps, 1922–26)

— WORLD CUP MASCOTS —

Every World Cup finals since 1966 has had an official mascot. These are the ones at the tournaments England qualified for:

Year	Host nation	Mascot	Description
1966	England	**World Cup Willie**	Lion playing football
1970	Mexico	**Juanito**	Sombrero-wearing boy
1982	Spain	**Naranjito**	Smiling orange
1986	Mexico	**Pique**	Chill pepper
1990	Italy	**Ciao**	Abstract figure with football for head
1998	France	**Footix**	Smiling cockerel
2002	Japan & Korea	**Kaz, Ato & Nik**	Three odd-looking creatures
2006	Germany	**Goleo VI & Pille**	Lion holding talking football

England have taken their own team mascots to two World Cups. In 1970, Sir Alf Ramsey's squad turned up in Mexico with a live bulldog, Winston (named after Winston Churchill). 12 years later, at the 1982 World Cup in Spain, England's mascot was the cartoon dog, Bulldog Bobby. Not everyone was happy with the choice, however, as there were concerns that the muscular figure in an England Admiral shirt sent out the wrong signals to some of the team's more aggressive fans.

— ENGLAND PLAYER OF THE YEAR —

Since 2003 England fans have been able to vote in an annual poll on the FA website for England's 'Player of the Year'. The winners to date are:

2003	David Beckham
2004	Frank Lampard
2005	Frank Lampard

In retaining his title in 2005, Lampard picked up 29% of the votes, while Steven Gerrard was second with 18% and Wayne Rooney third with 16%. Congratulating the Chelsea midfielder on his award, England manager Sven-Goran Eriksson said: "He is one of the most improved players I've seen in the last few years. He gets better and better. He has been brilliant for us in 2005."

— GLENN HODDLE'S FIRST ENGLAND TEAM —

Succeeding Terry Venables after Euro 96 at the age of 38, Glenn Hoddle was the youngest manager to take charge of England since Walter Winterbottom. Previously boss of Swindon and Chelsea, where he had built attractive sides generally employing a 3-5-2 formation, Hoddle promised to maintain the high standards of the Venables era. His first England selection, for a World Cup qualifier away to Moldova on 1st September 1996, was noteworthy for the international debut for a rising young star, one David Beckham (who played right wing-back). Here's how the team lined up:

1. **David Seaman** (Arsenal)
2. **Gary Neville** (Manchester United)
3. **Stuart Pearce** (Nottingham Forest)
4. **Paul Ince** (Inter Milan)
5. **Gary Pallister** (Manchester United)
6. **Gareth Southgate** (Aston Villa)
7. **David Beckham** (Manchester United)
8. **Paul Gascoigne** (Rangers)
9. **Alan Shearer** (Newcastle United, captain)
10. **Nick Barmby** (Middlesbrough)
11. **Andy Hinchcliffe** (Everton)

Substitutes: **David Batty** (Newcastle United) and **Matt Le Tissier** (Southampton)

— ENGLAND AT THE WORLD CUP: 1998 —

Having headed a tough World Cup qualifying group, which included Italy and Poland, England arrived in France for the tournament in confident mood. A comfortable opening game victory against Tunisia in Marseille was somewhat overshadowed by manager Glenn Hoddle's decision to leave both David Beckham and Michael Owen on the bench. Owen came on to score the equaliser against Romania a week later, but a last-minute goal by Chelsea's Dan Petrescu left England needing to beat Colombia in their final match to be certain of progressing. In the event, goals by Darren Anderton and Beckham, his first for his country, ensured the team would not be heading home early.

However, England's failure to top their group meant they were paired with tough opposition in the form of Argentina in the last 16. The match lived up to expectations, no more so than in the opening minutes which saw England fall behind to a penalty, then equalise through Shearer's spot-kick after Owen had been fouled in the box. The best was still to come, though, as Owen raced through the Argentine defence from a deep position before planting a firm shot past Carlos Roa for one of the most spectacular goals of the tournament. Before half-time, however, Javier Zanetti equalised for Argentina following a well-worked free-kick routine.

The rest of the match produced no more goals but plenty of controversy. Just after half-time Beckham was sent off after flicking out a boot at Diego Simeone. Down to ten men, England defended valiantly and seemed to have won the game when Sol Campbell headed in a corner, only for his 'goal' to be disallowed for a foul on the goalkeeper. After extra-time failed to provide a winner the game was decided on penalties. Seaman struck the first blow for England by saving from Hernan Crespo, but Roa responded by first palming away Paul Ince's effort and then blocking David Batty's weak penalty to put Argentina in the quarter-finals.

Group table

	P	W	D	L	F	A	Pts
Romania	3	2	1	0	4	2	7
England	3	2	0	1	5	2	6
Colombia	3	1	0	2	1	3	3
Tunisia	3	0	1	2	1	4	1

Date	Venue	Result
15th June 1998	Marseille	England 2 Tunisia 0
22nd June 1998	Toulouse	England 1 Romania 2
26th June 1998	Lens	England 2 Colombia 0
30th June 1998	St. Etienne (Last 16)	England 2 Argentina 2*^

* After extra time

^ Argentina won 4–3 on penalties

England squad: Tony Adams (Arsenal, 4 apps), **Darren Anderton** (Tottenham, 4 apps), **Sol Campbell** (Tottenham, 4 apps), **Paul Ince** (Liverpool, 4 apps), **Graeme Le Saux** (Chelsea, 4 apps), **David Seaman** (Arsenal, 4 apps), **Paul Scholes** (Manchester United, 4 apps), **Alan Shearer** (Newcastle United, 4 apps), **Gary Neville** (Manchester United, 3 apps), **David Batty** (Newcastle United, 2+2 apps), **Michael Owen** (Liverpool, 2+2 apps), **David Beckham** (Manchester United, 2+1 apps), **Teddy Sheringham** (Manchester United, 2 apps), **Gareth Southgate** (Aston Villa, 1+1 apps), **Rob Lee** (Newcastle United, 0+1 apps), **Steve McManaman** (Liverpool, 0+1 apps), **Paul Merson** (Middlesbrough, 0+1 apps), **Les Ferdinand** (Tottenham, 0 apps), **Rio Ferdinand** (West Ham United, 0 apps), **Tim Flowers** (Blackburn, 0 apps), **Martin Keown** (Arsenal, 0 apps), **Nigel Martyn** (Leeds United, 0 apps)

Goal scorers: Owen 2, Shearer 2, Anderton 1, Beckham 1, Scholes 1

Winners: France

They said it

"We had not practiced penalties in training, except for Alan Shearer, who always likes to."

Tony Adams, revealing a lack of preparation in the England camp

"The biggest mistake I made was not getting Eileen Drewey out to join us from the start."

Glenn Hoddle regrets not adding the faith healer to his squad

"I could have accepted it if we were beaten by a superior side. Another penalty shoot-out defeat was too much to take."

Alan Shearer on England's penalty shoot-out defeat by Argentina

— GET YOUR KIT ON —

'Home' kit

England's famous white shirts date back to the team's first game against Scotland in 1872. On that occasion the players wore white knickerbockers and while England have sometimes sported white shorts in the years since, more generally they have turned out in navy blue ones. The team's socks, meanwhile, have variously been white, navy blue or, for a short spell during the late 1950s and early 1960s, red.

For decades, England wore a traditional collared shirt with long sleeves that the players would typically roll up. Following the 6–3 and 7–1 thrashings in the 1953/54 season by the great Hungarian team of that period, England took a leaf from the 'Magical Magyars' book and introduced a new, lightweight shirt with a V-neck. This design was later adapted by Manchester-based company Umbro who began supplying the team with kit in the early 1960s.

In 1974 Admiral took over from Umbro as England's official suppliers, paying the FA an initial fee of £15,000 per year for the right to promote and sell replica kit. Admiral's first design was a controversial one, the red and blue striping on the collar and sleeve leading former England star Jimmy Greaves to declare that the kit looked like a 'pyjama top'. Sadly, the team provided some suitably sleepy performances in this era, failing to qualify for the finals of any major competition in the second half of the 1970s.

Umbro returned as official kit supplier in 1984 and has since produced a range of designs for the team. Innovations include the England badge moving to the centre of the shirt beneath the Umbro logo (1996) and a vertical red stripe appearing for the first time on the white shirt for Sven-Goran Erikkson's debut match as England manager in 2001.

'Away' kit

England's away kit has traditionally been red, although light blue or occasionally yellow have also been used. Most famously, England wore their second-choice red kit in the 1966 World Cup final against West Germany after losing the toss of a coin to decide which of the two sides would play in white. Other legendary games when England wore red include the 1970 World Cup quarter-final against West Germany, the 2002 World Cup defeat of Argentina and the World Cup qualifier against Germany in the last international at Wembley in 2000, when a conscious decision was taken by the FA to evoke the spirit of '66 in the choice of England's colours. Unfortunately, the ploy failed miserably, as England lost 1–0 and waved goodbye to their manager, Kevin Keegan, immediately afterwards.

The most controversial England away kit was the grey one (officially 'indigo blue') which Terry Venables' side wore against Germany in the Euro 96 semi-final at Wembley, despite a last-minute campaign among some fans and sections of the media for the team to revert to the classic red kit. UEFA deemed that England could not switch as the grey kit was their designated second choice for the tournament. Since then, however, and to the relief of most fans, a red kit has been restored as the team's preferred option in the case of a kit clash.

— NAMES AND NUMBERS —

Numbers first appeared on the back of England's shirts for the 3–1 defeat away to Scotland on 17th April 1937, two years before they became obligatory for Football League matches. England first wore squad numbers at the 1954 World Cup, while players' names first appeared on the back of shirts at the 1992 European Championships in Sweden. It wasn't until the famous 2–2 World Cup qualifying draw with Greece at Old Trafford in 2001, however, that England player names were printed on their shirts for a non-tournament match.

— CELEBRATING IN, ER, STYLE —

Unlike England's 2003 rugby union World Cup winners or the victorious 2005 Ashes cricketers, the World Cup heroes of 1966 did not celebrate their triumph with a huge public parade or a seven-day drinking binge. Instead, the post-match jollities were relatively muted:

Saturday evening, July 30th
After the match the squad is driven by coach from Wembley to the Royal Garden Hotel in Kensington High Street. The players appear on the hotel balcony to acknowledge the cheers of thousands of fans in the street below before attending a formal dinner. Labour Prime Minister Harold Wilson and Pickles, the dog that found the World Cup trophy, are among the VIP guests but, to the players' irritation, their wives are not invited to the function and dine instead in another part of the hotel. After the meal a number of players and their wives go out to Danny La Rue's club in Hanover Square.

Sunday lunchtime, July 31st

The players have Sunday lunch at the ATV studios in Boreham Wood, an event hosted by TV presenter Eamonn Andrews. Before the meal the players tell manager Alf Ramsey that they would like their £22,000 win bonus (on top of their match fees of £60 per game) to be split equally between all 22 members of the squad. After the meal the players, their lives changed forever, make their separate ways home.

— ENGLAND LEGENDS: TOM FINNEY —

Along with Stanley Matthews, Tom Finney was the outstanding footballer of his era. A supremely talented and pacy winger, he was equally effective on the right or left flank where his ability to cross the ball with either foot created countless chances for his team-mates. Unlike Matthews, Finney was also a regular goalscorer, finding the net an impressive 30 times in his 76 international appearances.

Nicknamed 'the Preston plumber' after an early apprenticeship, Finney played for the British Services XI during World War II while serving with the Tank Corps in the Middle East. He finally made his England debut in the first post-war international at the age of 24, scoring in a 7–2 rout of Northern Ireland in Belfast. He went on to star in some of the great England victories of the period, including the astonishing 10–0 thrashing of Portugal the following year and the famous 4–0 win over Italy in Turin in 1948.

Finney represented England at the 1950, 1954 and 1958 World Cups, although he only managed a single appearance at the last of these tournaments after becoming the victim of some brutal Russian tackling during a 2–2 draw in Gothenburg. A few months later Finney had his revenge, helping England beat the Soviets 5–0 at Wembley in his last international.

Tom Finney Factfile
Born: Preston, 5th April 1922
Club: Preston
Caps: 76 (1948–58)
Goals: 30
England debut: Northern Ireland 2 England 7, Belfast, 28th September 1946

Others on Finney

"No better player ever wore the white shirt. I was proud to have him as a colleague and as a friend."

Billy Wright

"When I told people in Scotland that England were coming up with a winger better than Stanley Matthews, they laughed at me. They weren't bloody laughing when Big Georgie Young was running all over Hampden looking for Tommy Finney."

Bill Shankly, a team-mate of Finney's at Preston

Tom Finney: 'The Preston Plumber'

— FATHERS AND SONS —

Just three sets of fathers and sons have both played for England. They are:

Father	Son
George R. Eastham	George E. Eastham
(1 cap, 1935)	(19 caps, 1963–66)
Brian Clough (2 caps, 1959)	Nigel Clough (14 caps, 1989–93)
Frank Lampard	Frank Lampard jnr
(2 caps, 1972–80)	(37 caps, 1999–)

— GRAHAM TAYLOR'S FIRST ENGLAND TEAM —

Previously the manager of Watford and Aston Villa, Graham Taylor succeeded Bobby Robson as England manager following the successful 1990 World Cup campaign. For his first match in charge, a Wembley friendly against Hungary on 12th September 1990 which England won 1–0, Taylor stuck to the old maxim 'If it ain't broke, don't fix it' and chose a team full of familiar names – and not a turnip in sight:

1. **Chris Woods** (Rangers)
2. **Lee Dixon** (Arsenal)
3. **Stuart Pearce** (Nottingham Forest)
4. **Paul Parker** (QPR)
5. **Des Walker** (Nottingham Forest)
6. **Mark Wright** (Derby County)
7. **David Platt** (Aston Villa)
8. **Paul Gascoigne** (Tottenham)
9. **Steve Bull** (Wolves)
10. **Gary Lineker** (Tottenham, captain)
11. **John Barnes** (Liverpool)

Substitutes: **Tony Dorigo** (Chelsea) and **Chris Waddle** (Marseille)

— WORLD CUP SONGS —

It's one of the oldest pub quiz questions in the book: which group topped the charts in 1970 and repeated the trick 20 years later with a completely different line up? The answer, of course, is the England World Cup squad whose various members enjoyed Number Ones with *Back Home* in 1970 and *World in Motion* in 1990 – although, in truth, that second success owed virtually everything to the quality of the song produced by Manchester band New Order.

Here is the full list of official England World Cup songs, from the chart-toppers to the ditties which (mercifully, some might say) sank without trace:

Year	Song	Artist	Highest Chart Position	Weeks in Chart
1970	*Back Home*	**England World Cup squad**	1	17
1982	*This Time (We'll Get It Right)*	**England World Cup squad**	2	13
1986	*We Got The Whole World At Our Feet*	**England World Cup squad**	66	2

1990	*World In Motion*	England/New Order	1	12
1998	*(How Does It Feel To Be)*	England United *On Top Of The World*	9	11
2002	*We're On The Ball*	Ant and Dec	3	11

In June 1996 England's official Euro 96 song, *Three Lions,* by comedians David Baddiel and Frank Skinner and the pop group The Lightning Seeds topped the charts for two weeks. The song, which looked back wistfully to England's 1966 heyday and famously described the intervening three decades of relative failure as '30 years of hurt', was not only a huge hit with the public but also with the players.

"I thought that Skinner and Baddiel's *Three Lions* encapsulated everything," wrote Stuart Pearce in his autobiography. "I remember the two comedians coming to the hotel and telling us this was going to be our song. They played it and we all shouted, 'rubbish, rubbish' but a couple of weeks later we were all singing it along with the rest of the nation."

— PENALTY SHOOT-OUT MISERY —

As every England fan surely knows, the national side has a desperately poor record in penalty shoot-outs in major tournaments. Well, 'poor' hardly does justice to England's spot-kick history which might better be summed up as 'miserable, dire and dismal'. Certainly, the stats make for grim reading: in five attempts since 1990, England have only managed one win – against Spain at Euro 96. The details of all the team's penalty shoot-out duels are given below:

Year	Tournament	Match Result	Shoot-out score	England players to miss
1990	World Cup	England 1 Germany 1	3–4	Stuart Pearce, Chris Waddle
1996	Euro 96	England 0 Spain 0	4–2	–
1996	Euro 96	England 1 Germany 1	5–6	Gareth Southgate
1998	World Cup	England 2 Argentina 2	3–4	Paul Ince, David Batty
2004	Euro 2004	England 2 Portugal 2	5–6	David Beckham, Darius Vassell

Of these England penalty-kick misses the ones by Waddle, Southgate, Batty and Beckham are probably the most infamous. Waddle's ballooned shot wide of the West German goal confirmed the Three Lions' exit from the 1990 World Cup and, 16 years on, remains an unhappy memory for many England fans. "A lot of people still come up and say, 'I'd never have taken one" and I say, 'I wish I hadn't'" said Waddle some years later. "There are two ways to react; basically you can do a Lord Lucan and disappear or stick your chest out and prove to everybody you're a good footballer." Waddle, it could be argued, followed both paths by returning to France to play his club football with Marseille.

Six years later international novice Gareth Southgate was the villain of the piece after his feeble penalty cost England a place in the final of Euro 96. Even his mother, Barbara, couldn't understand why he'd tried to place his kick, asking him, "Why didn't you just belt it, son?" Understandably, perhaps, with the press following his every move, Southgate chose the 'Lord Lucan' option. "I got away to Bali with my wife once we were knocked out and we found ourselves in a Buddhist temple, with these isolated lakes and volcanoes nearby," he recalled later. "Unfortunately I was spotted by a monk who told me, 'You Gareth Southgate, England penalty drama!'"

If Southgate was an unlikely penalty-taker, so too was David Batty. When the defensive midfielder stepped up to take a crucial penalty against Argentina at the 1998 World Cup not even his parents believed he would find the net. "Mary and I got the shock of our lives when David was asked to take a penalty," his father Al recalled later. "Neither of us really expected David to score." As every England fan knows, Batty snr and his wife were spot on – unlike their son.

At least David Beckham had some excuse – or so he said – when he sent his shoot-out spot-kick flying into the stands in the Euro 2004 shoot-out against Portugal. "I have watched my penalty on television and, when I plant my left foot to take the kick, you can see the ball lift up," complained the England captain. "I could not have hit the ball that way normally if I tried." The spongy pitch may have been fault but history still records that Beckham's penalty sailed into the stand behind the goal, the ball ending up in the hands of a fan in row Q. "I play basketball and when the ball came in my direction, I jumped, caught the ball with one hand and put it under my shirt," revealed 25-year-old Spaniard Pablo Carral. "I'm keeping it as a great trophy."

— SPOT-KICK AGONY AND ECSTASY —

Chris Waddle, England v West Germany, 1990 World Cup
Needing to score to keep England's hopes alive, Waddle takes a fast
bowler's run up but sends his kick high and wide of the goal.

Gareth Southgate, England v West Germany, Euro 1996
An inexperienced penalty taker, Southgate's weak shot is easily saved
by Koepke as he dives to his right.

David Batty, England v Argentina, World Cup 1998
Batty needs to score to keep England in the tournament, but his kick is too near the goalkeeper and Roa makes a comfortable save.

David Beckham, England v Portugal, Euro 2004
As Beckham runs in to shoot the ball moves slightly off the spot, leading the England captain to slice to slice his shot into the stands

— WORLD CUP QUALIFYING DISASTERS —

On three occasions England have plunged the nation into despair by failing to qualify for the World Cup.

In 1973 Sir Alf Ramsey's team needed to beat Poland at Wembley to book their place at the finals in West Germany the following year, but could only manage a 1–1 draw after an inspired display by the Polish goalkeeper, Jan Tomaszewski – a player dubbed 'The Clown' by TV pundit Brian Clough. Four years later England again missed out on World Cup qualification, despite being level on points with group winners Italy. Sadly for Ron Greenwood's men, the Italians had the better goal difference and so qualified for the finals in Argentina. Finally, Graham Taylor's England side completely botched up their qualifying group for the 1994 World Cup in the USA, and failed to grab either of the two available places. Away defeats to the two successful nations, Norway and Holland, were the pivotal moments in a campaign to forget.

World Cup year	Group rivals	Final nail-in-coffin result
1974	Poland, Wales	England 1 Poland 1
1978	Italy, Finland, Luxembourg	Italy 3 Luxembourg 0
1994	Norway, Holland Poland, Turkey, San Marino	Poland 1 Holland 3

— DON'T QUOTE ME 2 —

"He is a monument to something permanent in the English game: the Football Association's ability to cock up everything."

David Mellor on Sven-Goran Eriksson, 2006

"So he comes from Sweden. He could come from Mars as far as I'm concerned, as long as we win the World Cup."

Rio Ferdinand, backing Eriksson in 2001

"I'm fed up with him pointing to his grey hair and saying the England job has aged him 10 years. If he doesn't like it, why doesn't he go back to his orchard in Suffolk."

Brian Clough on Bobby Robson, 1983

"Even educated bees do it."

Brian Clough, exchange on ITV's World Cup panel, 1986

"England will never win World Cups. We simply don't have enough people who believe in playing football."

Alex Ferguson, 1995

"I used to quite like turnips, now my wife refuses to serve them."

Graham Taylor, 1995

"England had no direction but more formations than a ballroom dancing team."

Terry Butcher, unimpressed by England's defeat in Northern Ireland, 2005

"The good news is that Saddam Hussein is facing the death penalty. The bad news is that David Beckham's taking it."

Anonymous internet joke, after England's penalty shoot-out exit at Euro 2004

"There have, of course, been worse moments in English history – the Roman Conquest, the Black Death, the Civil War, the fall of France in 1940 and virtually the whole of the 1970s, for example."
The Times, putting England's 2002 World Cup failure in perspective

— WORLD CHAMPS DEFEATED —

On seven occasions England have beaten the reigning World Cup holders in high-profile friendlies. It's been a while, though, since our lads managed to pull this trick off: 1980, in fact, when two goals by Liverpool striker David Johnson and one by skipper Kevin Keegan saw off Argentina at Wembley.

Year	Venue	Result
1934	Highbury	England 3 Italy 2
1948	Turin	Italy 0 England 4*
1949	White Hart Lane	England 2 Italy 0*
1954	Wembley	England 3 West Germany 1
1956	Berlin	West Germany 1 England 3
1975	Wembley	England 2 West Germany 0
1980	Wembley	England 3 Argentina 1

* Italy were reigning holders from the last pre-war World Cup in 1938

— MUCH-TRAVELLED INTERNATIONALS —

Just two England players, Peter Shilton and David Platt, have been capped by their country while at five different clubs. The players' travels, however, couldn't have been more different, despite both starting off in the Midlands. While Shilton stayed close to his roots apart from an extended stop-off on the south coast, Platt's wanderings took in three Italian clubs before he hung up his boots at Arsenal.

Player	Clubs (with caps in brackets)
Peter Shilton	Leicester City (20), Stoke City (3), Nottingham Forest (19), Southampton (49), Derby County (34)
David Platt	Aston Villa (22), Bari (10), Juventus (10), Sampdoria (13), Arsenal (7)

— DOUBLE ENTENDRE XI —

Here's a team of risqué-sounding England internationals Julian Clary could have a lot of fun with (er, so to speak). And, talk of the devil, here is Julian to announce: "In a toss off . . . oops, I'll start again. In a toss up between the goalkeepers, Leslie Gay just beat off David Seaman . . ."

1. **Leslie Gay** (3 caps, 1893–94)
2. **Henry Cockburn** (13 caps, 1946–51)
3. **Charles Alcock** (1 cap, 1875)
4. **Nicky Butt** (39 caps, 1996–2004)
5. **Harold Hardman** (4 caps, 1905–08)
6. **Jimmy Dickinson** (48 caps, 1949–57)
7. **Ronald Dix** (1 cap, 1938)
8. **Alan Ball** (72 caps, 1965–75)
9. **Jack Cock** (2 caps, 1919–20)
10. **Hugh Adcock** (5 caps, 1929)
11. **Ellis Rimmer** (4 caps, 1930–31)

— ENGLAND AT THE WORLD CUP: 2002 —

Sven-Goran Eriksson's first tournament as England manager began disappointingly, with a lucklustre draw against his home nation, Sweden. Facing old enemies Argentina in their second match England responded with a much improved performance and deservedly triumphed after captain David Beckham drilled home a first-half penalty. Needing just a point to qualify for the knockout stages, England played out a drab goalless draw with Nigeria in the afternoon heat of Osaka.

The draw for the last 16 paired England with Denmark, surprise qualifiers with Senegal from World Cup holders France's group. The evening kick-off suited England far better, and the game was all but over by half-time when goals by Rio Ferdinand, Michael Owen and Emile Heskey had given Eriksson's team a commanding lead.

England's good form continued in the quarter-final against Brazil when Owen scored the opening goal midway through the first half. Just before half-time, though, Brazil's star player Ronaldinho set up Rivaldo for the equaliser and the initiative swung the way of the South Americans. Brazil's winning goal, a floated Ronaldinho free-kick which sailed over David Seaman's head, was something of a fluke but, frustratingly, England never looked like getting back in the game – even after Ronaldinho had been sent off. Ultimately, and to the intense disappointment of their many fans in Japan, England went out with a whimper rather than a bang.

Group table

	P	W	D	L	F	A	Pts
Sweden	3	1	2	0	4	3	5
England	3	1	2	0	2	1	5
Argentinia	3	1	1	1	2	2	4
Nigeria	3	0	1	2	1	3	1

Date	Venue	Result
2nd June 2002	Saitama	England 1 Sweden 1
7th June 2002	Sapporo	England 1 Argentina 0
12th June 2002	Osaka	England 0 Nigeria 0
15th June 2002	Niigata (Last 16)	England 3 Denmark 0
21st June 2002	Shizouka (Q/F)	England 1 Brazil 2

England squad: David Beckham (Manchester United, 5 apps), **Sol Campbell** (Arsenal, 5 apps), **Ashley Cole** (Arsenal, 5 apps), **Rio Ferdinand** (Leeds United, 5 apps), **Emile Heskey** (Liverpool, 5 apps), **Danny Mills** (Leeds United, 5 apps), **Michael Owen** (Liverpool, 5 apps), **Paul Scholes** (Manchester United, 5 apps), **David Seaman** (Arsenal, 5 apps), **Nicky Butt** (Manchester United, 4 apps), **Trevor Sinclair** (West Ham United, 3+1 apps), **Owen Hargreaves** (Bayern Munich, 2 apps), **Darius Vassell** (Aston Villa, 1+2 apps), **Teddy Sheringham** (Tottenham, 0+4 apps), **Kieron Dyer** (Newcastle United, 0+3 apps), **Wayne Bridge** (Southampton, 0+2 apps), **Joe Cole** (West Ham United, 0+1 apps), **Robbie Fowler** (Leeds United, 0+1 apps), **Wes Brown** (Manchester United, 0 apps), **David James** (West Ham United, 0 apps), **Martin Keown** (Arsenal, 0 apps), **Nigel Martyn** (Leeds United, 0 apps), **Gareth Southgate** (Middlesbrough, 0 apps)

Goal scorers: Owen 2, Beckham 1, Campbell 1, Ferdinand 1, Heskey 1

Tournament winners: Brazil

They said it

"They're better than us, which is the difference."
                    Sven Goran-Eriksson on England's conquerors Brazil

"Making a scapegoat out of 'Seamo' would be a disgrace. He has been the best keeper at the World Cup."
            England skipper **David Beckham** defending David Seaman
                            after the goalkeeper's blunder against Brazil

"All the European teams who have gone out played too defensive – like they were scared. I thought England were the worst."
South Korea coach **Gus Hiddink** on England's World Cup exit, 2002

— 10 GREATEST ENGLAND GOALS . . . EVER! —

In 2005, Sky One conducted a poll of England fans to find the best 50 goals in the country's history. Once the goals had been nominated they were then placed in their final positions by a panel of four judges: former England internationals Clive Allen and Alan Mullery, former Scotland striker Andy Gray and *Daily Telegraph* football writer Henry Winter. Here is the top 10:

1. Geoff Hurst, v West Germany, World Cup final 1966, Wembley
The third goal of a unique hat-trick, starting with a long pass from Bobby Moore which Hurst carried forward before unleashing a fierce left-foot shot high into the net.

2. Michael Owen, v Argentina, World Cup second round, 1998, St. Etienne
An astonishing individual goal, Owen beat three defenders for pace and then struck a high shot into the far corner.

3. David Beckham, v Greece, World Cup qualifier, 2001, Old Trafford
A curling, dipping free-kick from 25 yards which gave England a last-minute equaliser and guaranteed their qualification for the World Cup finals.

4. Paul Gascoigne, v Scotland, Euro 96, Wembley
Wide on the left, Gazza flicked the ball over the head of Scotland defender Colin Hendry before striking a low volley into the bottom corner.

5. John Barnes, v Brazil, friendly, Rio de Janeiro, 1984
Receiving the ball on the left wing, Barnes dribbled across the penalty area, beating four defenders and the goalkeeper before shooting into an unguarded net for a stunning individual goal.

6. Bobby Charlton, v Mexico, World Cup 1966, Wembley
A goal of immense power and accuracy, Charlton ran from the centre circle, swerved to the right to create space and hit a thunderous shot into the net from 25 yards.

7. Michael Owen, v Germany, World Cup qualifier, 2001, Munich
A composed finish in a one-on-one situation which sealed Owen's hat-trick during a famous team victory.

8. Steven Gerrard, v Germany, World Cup qualifier, 2001, Munich
A swerving low shot from 30 yards drilled just inside the post which gave England the lead in a vital World Cup qualifier.

9. Gary Lineker, v West Germany, World Cup semi-final 1990, Turin
A first touch to control the ball, then a typically accurate Lineker finish to provide England with a crucial equaliser in a closely-fought semi-final.

10. David Platt, v Belgium, World Cup second round, 1990, Bologna
A superbly executed swivel volley from Paul Gascoigne's floated free-kick to give England a last-minute winner.

— BILLY IS MR CONSISTENCY —

As well as being the first England player to win 100 international caps, the legendary Billy Wright holds the record for the most consecutive appearances for his country. After winning his 36th cap against France on 3rd October 1951 Wright went to play in every England game until his retirement from the pro game following the 8–1 defeat of the USA in Los Angeles on 28th May 1959 – an amazing total of 70 consecutive internationals.

— ENGLAND AT THE EUROPEAN CHAMPIONSHIPS: 1960–76 —

The European Championships failed to excite much interest when they began in 1960, England being one of a number of major football nations who declined to take part. The second tournament attracted wider participation, but England failed to get beyond the preliminary round, losing 6–3 on aggregate to France.

The Home International championships provided England's qualifying route to the latter stages of the 1968 competition. After defeating Spain 3–1 on aggregate in the quarter-finals, England joined hosts Italy, Yugoslavia and the USSR in the last four. Drawn against Yugoslavia, Sir Alf Ramsey's side went down 1–0 in Florence in a bruising encounter which ended with Alan Mullery becoming the first ever England player to be sent off. Three days later goals by Bobby Charlton and Geoff Hurst gave England victory over the USSR in a somewhat meaningless play-off to decide third and fourth place.

In 1972 England dropped just one point in qualifying for the quarter-finals ahead of Switzerland, Greece and Malta. Tougher opposition awaited, however, in the form of West Germany who, inspired by long-haired midfielder Gunter Netzer, won the first leg 3–1 at Wembley. Bizarrely, Ramsey chose an ultra-defensive side for the return in Berlin which finished in a 0–0 draw.

England's unhappy experience in the European Championships continued four years later when eventual winners Czechoslovakia pipped Don Revie's side for qualification by one point. Defeat against the Czechs in Bratislava didn't help England's cause, but ultimately two draws against third-placed Portugal were just as important a factor in the team's failure to progress to the finals in Yugoslavia.

— A MESSAGE FROM OUR SPONSORS —

The England team was first sponsored in 1994. Here is the complete list of sponsors and 'top tier partners' since then:

1994–98	Green Flag
1999–2002	Nationwide Building Society
2002–	Umbro, Nationwide Building Society, McDonald's, Carlsberg, Pepsi

Under FIFA regulations none of these sponsors' names or logos are allowed to appear on England's shirts. However, for the friendly against Holland at Villa Park on 9th February 2005 FIFA gave England permission to sport a slogan reading, 'No to Racism' in white letters across the chests of their red shirts and a 'Kick it Out' logo on the players' right sleeve as part of an anti-racist initiative. It was the first time any message or slogan had appeared on England's shirts, which normally just bear the Three Lions' crest, a small manufacturer's logo and the match fixture and date.

— SEEING RED —

Just nine players have been sent off while playing for England, and David Beckham is the only one of those to have been dismissed twice. The full list of England internationals who had first use of the showers is:

Date	Player	Match	Offence
5th June 1968	Alan Mullery	England 0 Yugoslavia 1	Retaliation
6th June 1973	Alan Ball	Poland 2 England 0	Violent conduct
12th June 1977	Trevor Cherry	Argentina 1 England 1	Foul play
6th June 1986	Ray Wilkins	England 0 Morocco 0	Two yellow cards
30th June 1998	David Beckham	England 2 Argentina 2	Retaliation
5th Sept 1998	Paul Ince	Sweden 2 England 1	Two yellow cards
5th June 1999	Paul Scholes	England 0 Sweden 0	Two yellow cards
8th Sept 1999	David Batty	Poland 0 England 0	Foul play
16th Oct 2002	Alan Smith	England 2 Macedonia 2	Two yellow cards
8th Oct 2005	David Beckham	England 1 Austria 0	Two yellow cards

— FALL GUY XI —

Lots of competition for places in this team of players all of whom boobed big-time in an England shirt:

1. David Seaman (75 caps, 1989–2002)
Let Ronaldinho's speculative long range free kick float over his head for Brazil's winner in the 2002 World Cup quarter-final. Remarkably, 'Safe Hands' repeated the trick just months later, completely missing a Macedonian corner which sailed into the net at the far post.

2. Phil Neville (52 caps, 1996–)
Conceded a last-minute penalty against Romania at Euro 2000 with a spectacularly mis-timed tackle. The Romanians scored from the spot and England were dumped out of the competition.

3. Stuart Pearce (78 caps, 1987–99)
According to Bobby Robson, the one player he was certain would score from the spot in England's 1990 World Cup semi-final penalty shoot-out was Stuart Pearce. As it turned out, 'Psycho' was the first England player to miss . . .

4. Norman Hunter (28 caps, 1966–75)
Completely failing to live up to his ferocious 'Bites Yer Legs' reputation, Norm lost a tackle on the halfway against Poland at Wembley in 1973. The Poles ran on to score and England were out of the World Cup before the tournament proper had even started.

5. Tony Adams (66 caps, 1987–2000)
Made to look a complete novice at the 1988 Euro championships by Dutch striker Marco van Basten, who helped himself to a hat-trick in England's 3–1 defeat.

6. Gareth Southgate (57 caps, 1995–2004)
Saw his feeble penalty – or was it a back pass? – saved by German keeper Andreas Koepke in the Euro 96 semi-final and then cashed in on his sudden notoriety with an inane ad for Pizza Hut

7. David Beckham (86 caps, 1996–)
Became 'Public Enemy Number One' after being sent off in the 1998 World Cup clash against Argentina for a petulant kick aimed at Diego Simeone. Six years later his reputation took another dive with a series of uninspiring displays at Euro 2004, capped by a grotesque penalty shoot-out miss in the quarter-final against Portugal.

8. Kevin Keegan (63 caps, 1972–82)
Injured for most of the 1982 World Cup, England skipper Kev recovered in time to come on as sub for the vital second round group game with hosts Spain. Presented with a gaping goal, Keegan somehow managed to put his header wide . . . and, minutes later, England were out of the tournament.

9. Jeff Astle (5 caps, 1969–70)
Coming on as a sub for England in the legendary match with Brazil at the 1970 World Cup, West Brom striker Astle had a great chance to equalise in the second half. Sad to say, he missed the target from just six yards out allowing Pele and co. to breathe again.

10. Geoff Thomas (9 caps, 1991–92)
Clean through against France at Wembley in 1992, the Crystal Palace midfielder tried to chip the advancing goalkeeper . . . only to slice his shot nearer the corner flag than the goal. Luckily for the hapless Thomas, it was only a friendly – but he still never played for England again.

11. Chris Waddle (62 caps, 1985–91)
Taking his team's last penalty in the 1990 World Cup semi-final shoot-out, Waddle had to score otherwise England were out. The situation demanded a cool head, but the Marseille winger was clearly a jumble of nerves as he dashed up to the ball and blasted his kick high into the night sky.

— UNBEATEN RUNS —

Way back in the late nineteenth century England put together a record run of 20 matches without defeat. The sequence began on 15th March 1889 in Belfast when England crushed Ireland 9–1 and continued until 16th March 1896 with, bizarrely enough, a victory by the same emphatic score over Wales in Cardiff. The seven-year run – which included 16 wins and four draws – finally came to an end in Glasgow on 4th April 1896 when Scotland beat England 2–1.

England's shock defeat was largely put down to an injury to the great Steve Bloomer, one of the legendary figures of the era. A forward with Derby, Bloomer scored an incredible 28 goals for England in 23 matches. His replacement for the Scotland game, Cuthbert James Burnup of Cambridge University, was a surprise one. Described later as 'painfully weak, almost everything he did ended in utter failure', Burnup was the archetype of the 'southern softie'. He never featured for England again, although playing cricket for MCC he set a record that still stands when he bowled a ball that was hit for 10 runs.

In the post-war period England went a record 19 matches without defeat (16 wins, three draws) between 10th November 1965 and 16th November 1966. The run was again ended by Scotland, who beat World Cup winners England 3–2 at Wembley on 15th April 1967. Scottish fans celebrated their triumph by running on to the pitch and taking away chunks of the turf as souvenirs – a practice the 'Tartan hordes' continued on their successful visits to Wembley in the 1970s.

— ENGLAND AT THE EUROPEAN CHAMPIONSHIPS: 1980 —

The format for the finals of the 1980 European Championships provided for two groups of four teams with the winners going directly into the final. Drawn with hosts Italy, Belgium and Spain, England began their campaign with a draw against the Belgians, in a match marred by crowd disturbances but illuminated by Ray Wilkins' cleverly lobbed goal. Three days later against Italy England boss Ron Greenwood continued his controversial policy of rotating his goalkeepers by bringing in Peter Shilton for Ray Clemence. Somewhat strangely, he also selected Nottingham Forest striker Garry Birtles, who was given a first start ahead of more established forwards. The changes couldn't prevent England going down to a defeat which signalled the end of their interest in the competition. A 2–1 victory over Spain in the final round of match was of little consequence, although it did ensure that England avoided finishing bottom of the group.

Group table

	P	W	D	L	F	A	Pts
Belgium	3	1	2	0	3	2	4
Italy	3	1	2	0	1	0	4
England	3	1	1	1	3	3	3
Spain	3	0	1	2	2	4	1

Date	Venue	Result
12th June 1980	Turin	England 1 Belgium 1
15th June 1980	Turin	Italy 1 England 0
18th June 1980	Naples	England 2 Spain 1

England squad: Kevin Keegan (Hamburg, 3 apps), **Phil Thompson** (Liverpool, 3 apps), **Dave Watson** (Southampton, 3 apps), **Ray Wilkins** (Manchester United, 3 apps), **Tony Woodcock** (Cologne, 3 apps), **Trevor Brooking** (West Ham United, 2 apps), **Ray Clemence** (Liverpool, 2 apps), **Steve Coppell** (Manchester United, 2 apps), **Phil**

Neal (Liverpool, 2 apps), **Kenny Sansom** (Crystal Palace, 2 apps), **Ray Kennedy** (Liverpool, 1+1 apps), **Terry McDermott** (Liverpool, 1+1 apps), **Viv Anderson** (Nottingham Forest, 1 app), **Garry Birtles** (Nottingham Forest, 1 app), **Glenn Hoddle** (Tottenham 1 app), **David Johnson** (Liverpool, 1 app), **Mick Mills** (Ipswich Town, 1 app), **Peter Shilton** (Nottingham Forest, 1 app), **Paul Mariner** (Ipswich Town, 0+2 apps), **Trevor Cherry** (Leeds United, 0+1 app), **Joe Corrigan** (Manchester City, 0 apps), **Emlyn Hughes** (Wolves, 0 apps)

Goal scorers: Brooking 1, Wilkins 1, Woodcock 1

Winners: West Germany

They said it:

"The troublemakers should be put on a boat and someone should pull the plug."

> **Ron Greenwood** slams the hooligans who shamed England in 'The Battle of Turin'

"England dominated large stretches of the match but we were rarely productive or destructive."

> **Peter Shilton** on the decisive defeat by Italy

— ARISE, SIR JOHN! —

It's often said that wing wizard Stanley Matthews was the first England footballer to be knighted but, in fact, this honour was originally bestowed on John Clegg, who appeared in the inaugural international between England and Scotland in 1872. Clegg later became a referee, officiating at the 1882 and 1892 FA Cup Finals, before becoming president of the FA from 1923 until his death in 1937. He was knighted in 1927. The full list of England internationals to get the sword-tapping treatment at Buck Pal reads:

Sir **John Charles Clegg** (Knighted 1927)
Sir **Stanley Matthews** (Knighted 1965)
Sir **Alf Ramsey** (Knighted 1967)
Sir **Walter Winterbottom** (Knighted 1978)
Sir **Bobby Charlton** (Knighted 1994)
Sir **Tom Finney** (Knighted 1998)
Sir **Geoff Hurst** (Knighted 1998)
Sir **Bobby Robson** (Knighted 2002)
Sir **Trevor Brooking** (Knighted 2004)

— 'LET'S ALL LAUGH AT SCOTLAND!' —

"I think Ally MacLeod [Scotland manager at 1978 World Cup] believes tactics are a new kind of peppermint."

Anon Scottish World Cup international, 1978

"It seems Charlie Nicholas is getting a lot of everything, except the ball."

Jimmy Greaves, 1984

"Hampden Park is the only ground which looks the same in black and white as it does in colour."

David Lacey, *The Guardian*, 1987

"The last time a team in Scotland lived up to expectations was in 1960 when Real Madrid beat Eintracht Frankfurt [in the European Cup Final] at Hampden Park."

Andy Roxburgh,1986

"He'd have a mixture of Billy Bremner arrogance – small and hard – Kenny Dalglish brilliance, Denis Law, the best-ever goalscorer, Dave Mackay, die-hard and desperate to win . . . and he'd have a pair of floppy hands."

Emlyn Hughes, on the ideal Scottish player, 1985

"I can't say England are shite because they beat us in the [Euro 2000] play-offs, and that would make us even shittier."

Ally McCoist, 2000

"We've been playing for an hour and it has just occurred to me that we're drawing 0–0 with a mountain top."

Ian Archer, Radio Scotland commentator, during a San Marino-Scotland match in 1993. Scotland eventually won 2–0.

"Where are the Jockos to replace the likes of Jim Baxter, who played a blinder when they beat us at Wembley in 1967? The only Baxter they've got up there now is a range of soups."

Jimmy Greaves, 1999

Reporter: "Welcome to Scotland."
Sir Alf Ramsey: "You must be f**king joking."

Exchange at Prestwick Airport when Ramsey arrived with the England team, 1968

— HURST'S HISTORIC HAT-TRICK —

As every schoolboy knows Geoff Hurst is the only player to have scored a hat-trick in a World Cup final. The England striker's three goals against West Germany in 1966 not only put him in the record books but, much more importantly, were instrumental in bringing the Jules Rimet trophy to these shores for the first, and so far only, time. In his autobiography *1966 and All That* (Headline, 2001) Hurst wrote at some length about the three goals that are forever associated with his name:

Goal 1, 19 minutes (1–1)
"The pass from Bobby (Moore) was perfection. I ran in from the right, met the ball with my head and steered it past Hans Tilkowski, the German goalkeeper."

Goal 2, 100 minutes (3–2)
"The ball was falling slightly behind me. I needed to adjust my body and take a couple of touches to get the ball into a shooting position. To get the power required to strike it properly, I had to fall back. As it turned out I connected beautifully with the ball but, in so doing, toppled over. I therefore had probably the worst view in the ground when the ball struck the underside of the bar and bounced down on the line."

Goal 3, 120 minutes (4–2)
"I decided to hit the ball with every last ounce of strength I had. I thought that if it flew over the bar and deep into the crowd it would waste a lot of time. Funnily enough, just as I shaped to kick the ball it hit a divot, bouncing up fractionally higher than I was anticipating. This meant that I caught it on the hard part of my instep and it flew into the net . . . Everybody went crazy, but I wasn't sure if it was a goal because the ref seemed to blow his whistle as the ball went in. When I realised it was a goal I was incredibly pleased."

Geoff Hurst's hat-trick made him a national institution

— ENGLAND AT THE EUROPEAN CHAMPIONSHIPS: 1988 —

Following an unbeaten qualifying campaign in which they had conceded just one goal, England arrived in Germany with high hopes of success. However, Bobby Robson's men got off to the worst possible start when they surprisingly lost 1–0 to the Republic of Ireland. Three days later a superb Dutch side featuring Marco van Basten, Ruud Gullit and Frank Rijkaard outclassed England in Dusseldorf, Van Basten claiming a hat-trick in the eventual champions' 3–1 win. A third defeat, this time against the Soviet Union, left England bottom of their group and rounded off a thoroughly depressing week. It later emerged that Gary Lineker was suffering from hepatitis during the tournament, a fact which accounted for some insipid displays by England's main striker. The rest of the squad, though, had no such excuses.

Group table

	P	W	D	L	F	A	Pts
USSR	3	2	1	0	5	2	5
Holland	3	2	0	1	4	2	4
Rep. Ireland	3	1	1	1	2	2	3
England	3	0	0	3	2	7	0

Date	Venue	Result
12th June 1988	Stuttgart	England 0 Rep. Ireland 1
15th June 1988	Dusseldorf	England 1 Holland 3
18th June 1988	Frankfurt	England 1 USSR 3

England squad: Tony Adams (Arsenal, 3 apps), **John Barnes** (Liverpool, 3 apps), **Gary Lineker** (Barcelona, 3 apps), **Bryan Robson** (Manchester United, 3 apps), **Kenny Sansom** (Arsenal, 3 apps), **Peter Shilton** (Derby County, 3 apps), **Gary Stevens** (Everton), **Glenn Hoddle** (Monaco, 2+1 apps), **Peter Beardsley** (Liverpool, 2 apps), **Trevor Steven** (Everton, 2 apps), **Mark Wright** (Derby County, 2 apps), **Chris Waddle** (Tottenham, 1+1 apps), **Neil Webb** (Nottingham Forest, 1+1 apps), **Steve McMahon** (Liverpool, 1 app), **Dave Watson** (Everton, 1 app), **Chris Woods** (Rangers, 1 app), **Mark Hateley** (Monaco, 0+3 apps), **Viv Anderson** (Manchester United, 0 apps), **Tony Dorigo** (Chelsea, 0 apps), **Peter Reid** (Everton, 0 apps)

Goal scorers: Adams 1, Robson 1

Tournament winners: Holland

They said it

"I felt we were more mature, more confident than in the 1986 World Cup in Mexico. My conviction was that we had a major chance of bringing the trophy home."

Bobby Robson

"We were, as a team, destroyed by the best striker in Europe."

Tony Adams, full of praise for Holland's Marco van Basten

— WALTZ ROUND VIENNA —

In May 1936 England travelled to Vienna to play a friendly against Austria, one of the leading sides of the inter-war era. On the morning of the match Austrian coach Hugo Meisl called at the England hotel and offered to give the visiting players a tour of the city.

"We jumped at the chance," recalled Eddie Hapgood, "and set off on what became the longest tour I have ever made of any city – on foot!" After leading them through Vienna's streets for miles, Meisl insisted on showing them the birthplace of the composer Johann Strauss, which he said was 'just round the corner'.

"It wasn't until 'the corner' had gone on for another two miles that we twigged and called off the trek," said Hapgood. "Otherwise we might still be wandering around Vienna."

Unsurprisingly, England's weary men lost 2–1, their first ever defeat to Austria.

— WILSON'S OWN GOAL —

In 1970 Labour Prime Minister Harold Wilson, a keen football fan, set the date of the General Election for June 18th, the day after the World Cup semi-final that most people expected holders England to win. Wilson was relying on the 'feelgood' factor to sweep him back into power but, instead, England lost their quarter-final to West Germany, the country was plunged into despair and come Election day Labour were narrowly defeated at the polls by Ted Heath's Conservatives. Wilson later reflected that England's surprise defeat had cost him his job.

— TAYLOR'S TURNIP PATCH —

Many England managers have been given a mauling by the press, but none have been quite so publicly mocked as Graham Taylor. The former Lincoln, Watford and Aston Villa boss's reign in charge of the national team got off to a decent start but after England lost to Sweden at the 1992 European Championships Taylor was subjected to a sustained press attack which only ended with his resignation in November 1993.

The Sun's famous response to that defeat in Stockholm, 'Swedes 2 Turnips 1' was aimed more at the players than the manager. The following day, however, Taylor's head was superimposed on a picture of a turnip and, among tabloid readers at least, the association of Taylor with the root vegetable stuck. He was, to all intents and purposes, Graham Taylor no more, simply 'The Turnip'.

While this was all rather unfortunate for the England manager, for the previously humble turnip the new nickname was a tremendous boon. With all the free publicity, sales of the vegetable soared. Some turnip-fanciers, however, were unimpressed. In a letter to the *Evening Standard* in 1992, Jon Meakin of the Fresh Fruit and Vegetable Association wrote:

> *"It's a shame they picked on the turnip. The turnip is a wonderful vegetable and it didn't do to do it down. If we were editing The Sun we would choose to compare the England team manager to a lesser known vegetable such as celeriac, okra or yam."*

The whole turnip saga was brought to an end when Taylor handed in his resignation after England's failure to qualify for the 1994 World Cup. Predictably, *The Sun* managed one last dig, hailing 'The Turnip's' departure with the memorable headline, 'That's Your Allotment'.

And it wasn't just *The Sun* who found Taylor a figure of fun:

"Hump it, bang it, whack it! It might be a recipe for a good sex life, but it won't win the World Cup."
Chelsea chairman Ken Bates on Taylor's long ball tactics

"As a vision of the future it ranks right up there alongside the SDP and the Sinclair C5."
Joe Lovejoy, of the Independent, on Taylor's stated intention to make England play a more direct game, 1992

"I heard that the Foreign Secretary's job has gone to Graham Taylor on the basis that if anyone could get us out of Europe he could."
Sir Ivan Lawrence, 1995

— THEY THINK IT'S ALL OVER —

"Some people are on the pitch. They think it's all over . . . it is now!" The words of BBC television commentator Kenneth Wolstenholme as Geoff Hurst scored England's fourth goal in the 1966 World Cup final have gone down in sporting history, been repeated more often than Winston Churchill's legendary "We'll fight them on the beaches" speech, provided the title for a long-running quiz show and an album by the band The Dentists, and been used by advertisers to flog everything from dog food to executive cars. Yet, at the time, the former bomber pilot's commentary barely registered with the TV audience, as Wolstenholme later recalled:

> *"I never realised my 1966 words would have such an impact. They didn't at the time. All the talk was about winning the World Cup and nobody gave a tupenny stuff what anyone had said on television or what the coverage had been like. But BBC2 repeated the match later in the year and it was after that, when people were watching it knowing the result, that the words came out and hit them. People rang me up and said, 'What were those words you said at the end?'"*

While Wolstenholme, who died at the age of 82 in 2002, is most often remembered for one snappy phrase at the end of English football's final hour (or, rather, two hours), it shouldn't be overlooked that he also came out with a couple of other memorable lines during the 1966 World Cup final:

"Yes, yes, yes . . . no! The linesman says no! The linesman says no. The linesman, who only speaks Russian and Turkish . . . it's a goal!"
(Describing the scenes as the referee and linesman consulted after Geoff Hurst's disputed third goal for England)

"It's only eight inches high, solid gold, and it means that England are the world champions."
(As The Queen presented England captain Bobby Moore with the Jules Rimet trophy)

— LOWER LEAGUE INTERNATIONALS —

Much as they might dream about playing for England, most pros at clubs like Chester, Torquay and Northampton will long ago have given up all hope of ever pulling on a shirt bearing the Three Lions badge. Yet, you never know, it may yet happen. Admittedly, it's a long shot, as since World War II only five players from outside the top two divisions have represented England at senior level. They are:

Year	Player	Club	Division
1948	Tommy Lawton	Notts County	Div Three (South)
1956	Reg Matthews	Coventry City	Div Three (South)
1962	Johnny Byrne	Crystal Palace	Div Three
1976	Peter Taylor	Crystal Palace	Div Three
1989	Steve Bull	Wolves	Div Three

— TERRY VENABLES' FIRST ENGLAND TEAM —

After the grey days of Graham Taylor's England reign, chirpy cockney Terry 'El Tel' Venables was the people's choice to lead the national side. For once, the blazered buffoons at FA headquarters took notice of public opinion and appointed the former QPR, Barcelona and Tottenham boss as England's first ever 'coach' (although, to all intents and purposes, he was still very much the manager). Typically, Venables' first England team was full of surprises, with debuts for Channel Islanders Graeme Le Saux and Matt Le Tissier, another for his Spurs protege Darren Anderton, and a recall after three years in the international wilderness for the evergreen Peter Beardsley. Here's how the side lined up for the 1–0 friendly win over Denmark at Wembley on 3rd April 1994:

1. **David Seaman** (Arsenal)
2. **Paul Parker** (Manchester United)
3. **Graeme Le Saux** (Blackburn Rovers)
4. **Paul Ince** (Manchester United)
5. **Gary Pallister** (Manchester United)
6. **Tony Adams** (Arsenal)
7. **David Platt** (Sampdoria, captain)
8. **Paul Gascoigne** (Lazio)
9. **Alan Shearer** (Blackburn Rovers)
10. **Peter Beardsley** (Newcastle United)
11. **Darren Anderton** (Tottenham)

Substitutes: **Matt Le Tissier** (Southampton) and **David Batty** (Leeds United)

— WINS AND DEFEATS: SOME FIRSTS —

First ever win: England 4 Scotland 2, Kennington Oval, 8th March 1873

First ever defeat: Scotland 2 England 1, Glasgow, 7th March 1874

First win against Wales: England 2 Wales 1, Kennington Oval, 18th January 1879

First defeat by Wales: England 0 Wales 1, Blackburn, 26th February 1881

First win over Ireland: Ireland 0 England 13, Belfast, 18th February 1882

First defeat by Ireland: Ireland 2 England 1, Belfast, 15th February 1913

First win against European opposition: Austria 1 England 6, Vienna, 6th June 1908

First defeat by European opposition: Spain 4 England 3, Madrid, 15th May 1929

First home win against European opposition: England 6 Belgium 1, Highbury, 19th March 1923

First home defeat by European opposition: England 3 Hungary 6, Wembley, 25th November 1953

First win over South American opposition: England 2 Chile 0, Rio de Janeiro, 25th June 1950

First defeat by South American opposition: Uruguay 2 England 1, Montevideo, 31st May 1953

First win over Asian opposition: England 1 Kuwait 0, Bilbao, 25th June 1982

First win over African opposition: England 1 Egypt 0, Cagliari, 21st June 1990

— TABLOID HELL —

The tabloid press in England has a love-hate relationship with the national football team. When the side is playing well or about to head off to a major tournament, there are no more enthusiastic cheerleaders than the 'red tops'. It's a very different story, though, when things are going badly as these damning headlines demonstrate:

Year	Match	Headline
1975	N. Ireland 0 England 0	'England – They're Just Irish Jokes' (*News of the World*)
1981	Switzerland 2 England 1	'End Of The World' (*Sunday Mirror*)
1986	England 0 Portugal 1	'World Cup Wallies' (*Daily Mirror*)
1988	England 0 Rep. Ireland 1	'On Yer Bike, Robson' (*The Sun*)

1988	England 1 USSR 3	'A Gutless Spineless Shower' (*The Sun*)
1988	Saudi Arabia 1 England 1	'In The Name Of Allah, Go!' (*The Sun*)
1992	Sweden 2 England 1	'Swedes 2 Turnips 1' (*The Sun*)
1992	Spain 1 England 0	'Spanish 1 Onions 0' (*The Sun*)
1993	Norway 2 England 0	'Norse Manure!' (*The Sun*)
1993	USA 2 England 0	'Yanks 2 Planks 0' (*The Sun*)
2005	Denmark 4 England 1	'Danish Pasting' (*The Mirror*)
2005	N. Ireland 1 England 0	'Taxi for Eriksson' (*The Sun*)

— ALL IN THE MIND —

Just occasionally, England have made use of some unconventional assistance from a variety of alternative healers, hypnotists and motivational gurus – with mixed results:

Olga Stringfellow, 1990

In a desperate bid to sort out his Achilles tendon, England captain Bryan Robson requested a faith healer to be flown out to the 1990 World Cup in Italy. Olga Stringfellow duly attempted to work her magic on the stricken midfielder, but to no avail: Robson failed to recover in time to play any further part in England's campaign.

Uri Geller, 1996 and 2002

If you believe Uri Geller, the famous spoon-bender and hypnotist, he was as much a part of England's famous Euro 96 win over Scotland as Paul Gascoigne, Alan Shearer or any other member of Terry Venables' team.

With England leading 1–0 in the second half, Scotland were awarded a penalty. It was at this point that Geller, who was circling Wembley in a helicopter at the time, claims to have used his mind-over-matter powers to make the ball move slightly just as Gary McAllister ran in to take his kick. "I made the ball move a bit by mind power," he said later. "It stopped McAllister scoring." Maybe, but even Geller would probably admit that England goalkeeper David Seaman, who brilliantly palmed away McAllister's fiercely struck shot, played some role in the Scots' failure to equalise.

Fast forward six years and Geller was back in the news again when he claimed he could heal David Beckham's injured foot ahead of the 2002 World Cup. "I'm not a miracle worker, but if millions of people focus their minds on David's foot and visualize the bone knitting together we can unleash a powerful healing force," he told GMTV viewers. "I want people to touch their TV screens. Take it seriously, if just for a few seconds, and send him some healing energy." Sure enough, Becks was fit for the tournament. But, England fans might have wondered, what happened to Geller's ball-moving powers when Ronaldinho ran in to take that free-kick in the England-Brazil match?

Eileen Drewery, 1996–99

Famously, former Essex pub landlady turned faith healer Eileen Drewery was a key member of the England inner sanctum during Glenn Hoddle's period as manager. A room was put aside for her in the team's hotel in Burnham Beeches, near Maidenhead, and the squad were told that she would be available if any player thought an injury could be cured by faith healing. Hoddle also said players should go and see her if they needed counselling for any personal problems. Some England players, such as Darren Anderton, felt they were helped by their sessions with Drewery but others treated her as a joke figure. Ray Parlour was one player who didn't take her seriously. When Drewery put her hands on his head and asked him what he wanted he replied, "A short back and sides, please."

— SHILTS' APPEARANCE RECORD —

With 125 caps to his name goalkeeper Peter Shilton is easily England's most-capped player. First selected by Sir Alf Ramsey for a friendly match against East Germany at Wembley in 1970, Shilton made his last appearance for England a full 20 years later at the 1990 World Cup. His record tally would have been much higher if for many years he hadn't been competing for the England keeper's jersey with Ray Clemence, who won over 60 caps between 1972 and 1983.

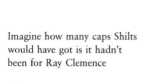

Imagine how many caps Shilts would have got is it hadn't been for Ray Clemence

The players who have won most caps for England are:

Player	Caps	Years
Peter Shilton	125	1970–90
Bobby Moore	108	1962–73
Bobby Charlton	106	1958–70
Billy Wright	105	1947–59
Bryan Robson	90	1980–91
David Beckham	86	1996–
Kenny Sansom	86	1979–88
Ray Wilkins	84	1976–86
Gary Lineker	80	1984–92

— WHO'S IN GOAL NEXT? —

Rather like a disorganised Sunday League team England struggled to find a regular goalkeeper in the early days of the national team. Indeed, in the first nine games England played no fewer than 10 players took up position between the sticks (for the very first game against Scotland in 1872, Robert Barker and William Maynard each played a half in goal and a half on pitch. The first keeper to line up more than once for England was Harry Swepstone of Pilgrims FC, who made six appearances between 1880 and 1883.

— THE 100 CLUB —

Although David Beckham and Gary Neville may soon join them, only four players have so far made 100 or more appearances for England: Billy Wright, Bobby Charlton, Bobby Moore and Peter Shilton. The matches when the quartet of centurions reached the landmark figure are listed below:

Player	Date	Venue	Match result
Billy Wright	11th April 1959	Wembley	England 1 Scotland 0
Bobby Charlton	21st April 1970	Wembley	England 3 Northern Ireland 1
Bobby Moore	14th Feb 1973	Hampden Park	Scotland 0 England 5
Peter Shilton	15th June 1988	Dusseldorf	England 1 Holland 3

— CAPPED ABROAD XI —

Unsurprisingly, the vast majority of players to represent England have done so while appearing for clubs in this country. A small minority (26 in total), however, have been called up for international duty while playing for non-English clubs, including this team of foreign-based players:

1. **Chris Woods** (Glasgow Rangers, 20 caps, 1986–91)
2. **Des Walker** (Sampdoria, 11 caps, 1992–93)
3. **Dave Watson** (Werder Bremen, 1 cap, 1979)
4. **David Platt** (Bari, Juventus and Sampdoria, 33 caps, 1991–95)
5. **Ray Wilkins** (AC Milan, 22 caps, 1984–86)
6. **Glenn Hoddle** (Monaco, 9 caps, 1987–88)
7. **Kevin Keegan** (Hamburg, 26 caps, 1977–80)
8. **Tony Woodcock** (Cologne, 18 caps, 1979–82)
9. **Gary Lineker** (Barcelona, 24 caps, 1986–89)
10. **Joe Baker** (Hibs, 5 caps, 1960)
11. **Chris Waddle** (Marseille, 18 caps, 1989–91)

— CAPTAIN MARVELS —

When David Beckham led out England for the prestigious international friendly against Argentina in Geneva in November 2005 it was the 50th time that he had captained his country. Incredibly, though, Becks is still only just over halfway to matching the records set by Billy Wright and Bobby Moore, both of whom skippered England on 90 occasions. Altogether, 105 players have captained England since Cuthbert Ottaway first had the honour against Scotland in 1872 – although 39 of them only did so on one occasion. More regular skippers include:

Player	Years	Caps won as captain
Billy Wright	1948–59	90
Bobby Moore	1963–73	90
Bryan Robson	1982–91	65
David Beckham	2000–	50*
Alan Shearer	1996–2000	34
Kevin Keegan	1976–82	31
Emlyn Hughes	1974–80	23
Johnny Haynes	1960–62	22
Eddie Hapgood	1934–39	21

— GREAVSIE'S HAT-TRICKS —

No player has scored more hat-tricks for England than Jimmy Greaves. The incomparable goal poacher took home the match ball six times after playing for his country:

Date	Venue	Result	Greaves goals
19th Oct 1960	Luxembourg	Luxembourg 0 England 9	3
15th April 1961	Wembley	England 9 Scotland 3	3
20th May 1962	Lima	Peru 0 England 4	3
20th Nov 1963	Wembley	England 8 N Ireland 3	4
3rd Oct 1964	Belfast	N Ireland 3 England 4	3
29th June 1966	Oslo	Norway 1 England 6	4

— ENGLAND LEGENDS: ALAN SHEARER —

Tommy Lawton, Nat Lofthouse and Geoff Hurst all have a claim to the title, but few would dispute that England's finest ever centre forward is Alan Shearer. During his eight-year international career the Geordie number nine picked up where his predecessor Gary Lineker left off, scoring goals against some of the world's best and most highly-organised teams.

Shearer's high watermark in an England shirt was Euro 96 when his partnership with Teddy Sheringham was his country's main source of goals. While Sheringham probed and schemed, Shearer was altogether more forceful: using his powerful physique to ruffle defenders, and emphatically burying any chances that came his way. One of his two goals against Holland, when he almost broke the Dutch net with a hammer-like rising shot, summed up Shearer's old-fashioned, uncomplicated approach to goalscoring. Even his trademark goal celebration, an arm raised skywards, seemed to belong to an earlier, more simple age. The England fans loved him, though, and chants of 'Shear-er, Shear-er!' poured down from the Wembley stands at home games.

Shearer was appointed England captain by Glenn Hoddle in 1996, a role he performed at the 1998 World Cup and maintained when Kevin Keegan took over as manager. Shearer's last international tournament was the 2000 European Championships when, despite taking his England goal tally to 30 with strikes against Germany and Romania, he couldn't save his side from early elimination. Nonetheless, it is a sign of the respect in which Shearer is held that there have been repeated calls for him to reconsider his retirement and return to the England fold.

Alan Shearer Factfile
Born: Newcastle, 13th August 1970
Clubs: Southampton, Blackburn Rovers, Newcastle United
Caps: 63 (1992–2000)
Goals: 30
England debut: England 2 France 0, 19th February 1992
International honours: England captain 34 times (1996–2000), Golden Boot (Euro 96)

Others on Shearer

"He is very determined in the box and very aggressive. He is, simply, an all-round centre-forward and a good leader, too."

England team-mate **Tony Adams**

"He's a real man and a leader. I don't think there's another Alan Shearer in England."

Kevin Keegan paying tribute to Shearer after he announced his retirement from international football in 2000

Alan Shearer's goals were more exciting than his celebrations

— ENGLAND MANAGERS' RECORDS —

Including three caretaker managers, 13 men have taken charge of the national team since the selection committee handed over their responsibilities to Walter Winterbottom after World War II. Their varying records in the England hotseat are as follows:

Manager	P	W	D	L	F	A	win %
Walter Winterbottom 1946–62)	139	78	33	28	383	196	56.11
Alf Ramsey (1963–74)	113	69	27	17	224	98	61.06
Joe Mercer (1974)*	7	3	3	1	9	7	42.85
Don Revie (1974–77)	29	14	8	7	49	25	48.27
Ron Greenwood (1977–82)	55	33	12	10	93	40	59.99
Bobby Robson (1982–90)	95	47	30	18	154	60	49.47
Graham Taylor (1990–93)	38	18	13	7	62	32	47.36
Terry Venables (1994–96)	23	11	11	1	35	13	47.82
Glenn Hoddle (1996–1999)	28	17	6	5	42	13	60.71
Howard Wilkinson (1999, 2000)*	2	0	1	1	0	2	0.00
Kevin Keegan (1999–2000)	18	7	7	4	26	15	38.88
Peter Taylor (2000)*	1	0	0	1	0	1	0.00
Sven-Goran Eriksson (2001–)	59	34	15	10	111	57	57.63

* Caretaker manager

— 1,000 UP —

Neil Webb of Nottingham Forest became the 1,000th player to be used by England when he came on as a substitute for Glenn Hoddle during the 3–1 defeat to West Germany in Dusseldorf on 9th September 1987. Twenty seven years earlier, on 23rd November 1960, Jimmy Greaves scored England's 1,000th goal in the Three Lions' 5–1 win over Wales at Wembley.

— SILLY NAME XI —

England have been blessed over the years with numerous players who rejoice in some pretty strange surnames including, as it happens, 'Strange'. Herod Ruddlesdin and Segal Bastard are the pick of this side for having nutty Christian names as well as oddball surnames. What on earth were their parents thinking of?

1. **A.H. Savage** (1 cap, 1876)
2. **Edwin Mosscrop** (2 caps, 1914)
3. **Ernest Blenkinsop** (26 caps, 1928–33)
4. **Alfred Strange** (20 caps, 1930–33)
5. **Harold Pantling** (1 cap, 1923)
6. **Francis Cuggy** (2 caps, 1913–14)
7. **Herod Ruddlesdin** (3 caps, 1904–05)
8. **Sydney Puddefort** (2 caps, 1925–26)
9. **William Spouncer** (1 cap, 1900)
10. **Harry Daft** (5 caps, 1889–92)
11. **Segal Bastard** (1 cap, 1880)

— BLACK IN WHITE —

Although he never played in a full international, Stoke's Frank Soo can claim to be the first non-white player to represent England at football. Soo, who was of mixed English and Chinese parentage, played in nine wartime internationals for England between 1942 and 1945.

The first black player to represent England in a full international was Nottingham Forest full-back Viv Anderson, who proudly pulled on the Three Lions shirt for the visit of Czechoslovakia to Wembley on 29th November 1978. He later downplayed the significance of his selection, saying, "Whether you are white, brown, purple or blue it's the same. When you are fortunate enough to make an England debut at Wembley it's the greatest feeling in the world." Even better, England won the game 1–0.

15 years later, on 9th June 1993, Paul Ince became the first black player to captain England when Graham Taylor handed him the armband for the friendly fixture with the USA in the Foxboro Stadium, Boston. It wasn't the happiest of occasions, however, as England surprisingly lost 2–0.

— THE HOME INTERNATIONAL CHAMPIONSHIP: RECORDS —

England tournament outright wins: 34 (Scotland 24, Wales 7, Northern Ireland 3)
Shared wins: 20

Record wins

Date	Venue	Result
16th March 1896	Cardiff	Wales 1 England 9
18th Feb 1899	Sunderland	England 13 Ireland 2
15th April 1961	Wembley	England 9 Scotland 3

Record defeats

Date	Venue	Result
14th Feb 1914	Middlesbrough	England 0 Ireland 3
31st March 1928	Wembley	England 1 Scotland 5
17th May 1980	Wrexham	Wales 4 England 1

Most consecutive titles won: 10 (including 6 shared), 1951/52–1960/61
Most consecutive seasons without a title win: 8, 1913/14–1925/26
Most consecutive games undefeated: 20 (1890–1896)
Most consecutive games without a win: 5 (1923–24)
Most goals scored in a season: 19, in 1899
Fewest goals scored in a season: 0, in 1981 (two matches only)
Fewest goals conceded in a season: 0, in 1909 and 1982
Most goals conceded in a season: 9, in 1927/28
Most appearances: Billy Wright, 38 (1947–59)
Most goals scored: Steve Bloomer, 28 (1895–1907)

— THE NAME GAME —

A team of England internationals with unusual middle names:

1. Arnold **Oak** Scattergood (1 cap, 1913)
2. Ledley **Brenton** King (15 caps, 2002–)
3. Graeme **Pierre** Le Saux (36 caps, 1994–2000)
4. Paul **Emerson Carlyle** Ince (53 caps, 1992–2000)
5. Sol **Jeremiah** Campbell (66 caps, 1996–)
6. Martin **Stanford** Peters (67 caps, 1966–74)
7. Luther **Loide** Blissett (14 caps, 1982–84)
8. Eric **Lazenby** Gates (2 caps, 1980)
9. Emile William **Ivanhoe** Heskey (43 caps, 1999–2004)
10. Martin **Harcourt** Chivers (24 caps, 1971–73)
11. Derek **Tennyson** Kevan (14 caps, 1957–61)

— LONE INTERNATIONAL —

Among current Premiership and Football League clubs five have provided the England team with just a single international player:

Club	Player	Caps won	Year(s)
Barnsley	George Utley	1	1913
Bristol Rovers	Geoff Bradford	1	1955
Crewe Alexandra	John Pearson	1	1892
Stockport County	Henry Hardy	1	1924
Swindon Town	Harold Fleming	11	1909–14

— GOAL SHY DEFENDERS —

Among outfield players, Gary Neville holds the England record for having played the most games for his country without scoring a single goal. Strangely (or not), his brother Phil also features in the all-time top five for this particular category. Must be something in the genes . . .

Player	Years played	Caps	Goals
Gary Neville	1995–	77	0
Ray Wilson	1960–68	63	0
Des Walker	1988–93	59	0
Phil Neville	1996–	52	0
Jimmy Dickinson	1949–56	48	0

— BALL AND BAT: DOUBLE INTERNATIONALS —

A selection of England internationals who also played cricket for the Three Lions:

Player	Football caps	Cricket caps
C.B. Fry	1 (1901)	26 (1896–1912)
Billy Gunn	2 (1884)	11 (1887–99)
Harry Makepeace	4 (1906–12)	4 (1920–21)
Willie Watson	4 (1949–50)	23 (1951–59)
Arthur Milton	1 (1952)	6 (1958–59)
'Tip' Foster	5 (1900–02)	8 (1903–07)

Denis Compton, who played cricket for England between 1937 and 1957, is often mentioned as a 'double international', but his 12 England football caps were all won in wartime internationals which don't count in official records.

— GOING ONCE . . . —

A number of England's 1966 heroes have, for various reasons, decided to put their World Cup winners' medals up for sale:

George Cohen The first member of the '66 team to put his medal up for auction, Cohen was disappointed when bids failed to reach the £60,000 reserve price in 1998.

Bobby Moore Seven years after his death in 1993, Moore's ex-wife Tina sold a collection of his football memorabilia, including his World Cup medal, to his former club West Ham for a total of £150,000.

Geoff Hurst Sold his medal, along with other items of football memorabilia, to his old club West Ham in 2000 for £150,000.

Gordon Banks In March 2001 Banks sold his medal at auction for £124,750.

Ray Wilson The Huddersfield Town left-back sold his medal for £80,000 in 2002.

Alan Ball In an auction at Christie's in May 2005 Bally's World Cup medal fetched a record £164,800.

— WEMBLEY DEBUT —

Built by Sir Robert McAlpine & sons of Pall Mall, London and designed by architects John Simpson and Maxwell Ayrton, the original Wembley stadium was constructed in just 300 days in 1922 and 1923 at a cost of £750,000. More than 25,000 tons of concrete, 1,500 tons of steel girders and 500,000 rivets were used in the building of the stadium, which included two 126-feet white towers which would rapidly become a famous London landmark. Curiously, a train lay under the pitch after being left there during the stadium's construction.

England's first game at Wembley was against Scotland on 12th April 1924, a year after the new stadium was swamped by enthusiastic fans for its opening match, the 1923 FA Cup Final between Bolton and West Ham. Perhaps put off by the scenes of chaos at that game – play was only possible when a policeman on a white horse cleared the pitch of spectators – the attendance for the first international at the Twin Towers, which finished in a 1–1 draw, was just 37,250.

In the years before the Second World War the only internationals played at Wembley were England's home meetings with Scotland. Other fixtures were held at a variety of venues, including Highbury, Stamford Bridge and St James' Park. After the war this tradition was continued, but by the early 1950's an increasing number of England matches were being held at Wembley and, within a few years, the stadium was adopted as England's primary 'home'.

One of the famous Twin Towers

Wembley debuts

Date	Team	Result
12th April 1924	Scotland	England 1 Scotland 1
9th May 1951	First overseas team	England 2 Argentina 1
28th Nov 1951	First continental team	England 2 Austria 2
12th Nov 1952	Wales	England 5 Wales 2
2nd Nov 1955	Northern Ireland	England 3 Northern Ireland 0

— SPORTING VARIETY —

Other sports staged at Wembley:

Athletics, including the 1948 Olympic Games
Greyhound racing (first staged 1927)
Rugby (first Five Nations game, Wales v Scotland in 1998)
Rugby League (Cup final first staged 1929)
Speedway (1931–1981)
American Football (Dallas Cowboys v Chicago bears exhibition game, 1986)

— ENGLAND AT THE EUROPEAN CHAMPIONSHIPS: 1992 —

Hit by injuries and lacking a recognised right-back, England travelled to Sweden with a decidedly mediocre-looking squad. Controversially, manager Graham Taylor had ignored the claims of a trio of genuinely international class players in Peter Beardsley, Chris Waddle and Ian Wright, preferring instead the more prosaic talents of long-limbed midfield hustler Carlton Palmer and inconsistent winger Tony Daley. Two dull 0–0 draws with eventual winners Denmark and France were followed by a must-win game against the hosts. David Platt gave England the lead, but the Swedes levelled before half-time. With half an hour remaining Taylor substituted his captain and most likely scorer Gary Lineker, playing in his last England match, but it was Sweden who went on to score a winner. The headlines the next day made grim reading for Taylor.

Group table

	P	W	D	L	F	A	Pts
Sweden	3	2	1	0	4	2	5
Denmark	3	1	1	1	2	2	3
France	3	0	2	1	2	3	2
England	3	0	2	1	1	2	2

Date	Venue	Result
11th June 1992	Malmo	England 0 Denmark 0
14th June 1992	Malmo	England 0 France 0
17th June 1992	Stockholm	Sweden 2 England 1

England squad: Martin Keown (Everton, 3 apps), **Gary Lineker** (Tottenham, 3 apps), **Carlton Palmer** (Sheffield Wednesday, 3 apps), **Stuart Pearce** (Nottingham Forest, 3 apps), **David Platt** (Bari, 3 apps), **Chris Woods** (Sheffield Wednesday, 3 apps), **David Batty** (Leeds United, 2 apps), **Andy Sinton** (QPR, 2 apps), **Trevor Steven** (Marseille, 2 apps), **Tony Daley** (Aston Villa, 1+1 apps), **Paul Merson** (Arsenal, 1+1 apps), **Alan Smith** (Arsenal, 1+1 apps), **Neil Webb** (Manchester United, 1+1 apps), **Keith Curle** (Manchester City, 1 app), **Alan Shearer** (Southampton, 1 app), **Nigel Clough** (Nottingham Forest, 0 apps), **Tony Dorigo** (Leeds United, 0 apps), **Nigel Martyn** (Crystal Palace, 0 apps), **Mark Wright** (Liverpool, 0 apps)*
* withdrew from squad injured

Goal scorer: Platt 1

Tournament winners: Denmark

They said it

"It was not Gary's type of game and I wanted someone who could hold the ball for us up front."

> **Graham Taylor**, explaining his controversial substitution of Gary Lineker in England's defeat against Sweden

"In truth, we were a few players short of being a good team and we didn't play well in the tournament. There was certainly something missing."

> **Stuart Pearce**, making no excuses for England's disappointing showing

— UNKNOWN QUANTITY —

Owen Hargreaves is the only player to have been capped by England who has never played for an English club. The Canadian-born midfielder has won all of his 29 international caps whilst with German giants Bayern Munich, his only professional club to date.

Apart from Hargreaves, just two England players have won all their caps while playing for non-English teams. However, Mark Walters (capped once with Rangers in 1991) and Alan Thompson (capped once with Celtic in 2004) had both previously played in the English league.

— WEMBLEY INTERNATIONAL . . . BUT NO THREE LIONS —

However unlikely it sounds, five internationals have been played at Wembley – the home of English football – without England being involved. Three of the games took place during the 1966 World Cup when the stadium was used as the main venue for matches in England's group. Wembley was also the venue for the finals of the 1948 Olympic Games and Euro 96. Here are the details of those England-less games:

Date	Occasion	Result
13th Aug 1948	Olympic final	Sweden 3 Yugoslavia 1
13th July 1966	World Cup group match	France 1 Mexico 1
19th July 1966	World Cup group match	Uruguay 0 Mexico 0
28th July 1966	World Cup 3rd/4th play-off	Portugal 2 USSR 1
30th June 1996	Euro 96 final	Germany 2
		Czech Republic 1*

* Germany won on 'golden goal' rule

— ENGLAND LEGENDS: DAVID BECKHAM —

Although David Beckham's international days are far from over, it is surely not too early to elevate Sven-Goran Eriksson's captain to the pantheon of all-time England greats. Forget the tabloid hype surrounding one of the planet's most recognisable celebrities, judged solely as a footballer Beckham is a talent of the very first order.

To a remarkable extent, the well-chronicled ups-and-downs of Beckham's England career have mirrored those of the international team: in 1998, the midfielder was a very public scapegoat for his country's failure at the World Cup in France, after his immature reaction to a foul by Argentina's Diego Simeone led to his dismissal; three years later, he was hailed as a hero as his magnificent last-minute free-kick against Greece guaranteed England's qualification for the 2002 World Cup, then, at the tournament proper, it was his confidently struck penalty that gave England revenge against Argentina and provided Beckham with a glorious moment of personal redemption. Fast forward two years and Beckham was again the villain of the piece, ballooning a penalty into the night sky as England crashed out of the European championships in Portugal.

While the spotlight has remained more firmly fixed on him than any other England player, Beckham's form for his country has rarely dipped below the high standards he sets for himself. A superb passer of the ball from central or wide areas, a magnificent crosser and a (usually) deadly striker of set-pieces, even in his thirties Beckham is still a central figure in the England set-up. All that remains is for the boy from Leytonstone to emulate another legendary east Londoner, Bobby Moore, and lift some serious international silverware.

David Beckham Factfile
Born: Leytonstone, 2nd May 1975
Clubs: Manchester United, Real Madrid
Caps: 86 (1996–)
Goals: 16
England debut: Moldova 0 England 3, 1st September 1996
International honours: England captain 50 times (2000-present)

Others on Beckham
"David Beckham has charisma. If he were in this room, we would all be looking at him. That's something you're born with."

Sven-Goran Eriksson

"David Beckham is the only British player who would get into the Brazilian squad."

Rivaldo, Brazilian World Cup star

David Beckham has captained England 50 times
despite only having one leg!

— COMPLETELY UNOFFICIAL —

Over the years England have played a number of unofficial matches, either against other countries or, occasionally, club sides. Here is a selection of results from these matches:

Date	Venue	Result
5th March 1870	Kennington Oval	England 1 Scotland 1
19th December 1891	Kennington Oval	England 6 Canada 1
21st March 1934	Roker Park	England 1 Rest of England 7
4th June 1969	Guadalajara	Mexico 0 England 4
4th February 1975	White Hart Lane	Tottenham 2 England 0
5th June 1990	Oristano	Sardinian XI 2 England 10
26th May 1996	Hong Kong	Hong Kong Golden Select 0 England 1
9th June 1998	Caen	Caen 0 England 1

Of these games, there was an extraordinary incident in the one England played in Sardinia shortly before the start of the 1990 World Cup. From the kick-off, Steve McMahon took the ball down the pitch and blasted it into the England net to score a deliberate own goal. The stadium announcer then informed the confused fans that McMahon's apparently bonkers action was a symbolic message to them: that violence was an 'own goal'. Fortunately, England didn't try to drill home the anti-hooligan point in the same way once the World Cup actually started.

— "ENGLAND, MY ENGLAND" —

Three Lions-related quotes from the autobiographies of the stars:

"I have been asked a few times by journalists, 'Where were you the day we beat West Germany in the World Cup?' and I've always answered, 'I can't remember.' I can though. I was in Lesley's flat in West Hampstead, in bed with Lesley, watching it on television."

Actor **Rodney Bewes**, *A Likely Story: the autobiography of Rodney Bewes* (Century, 2005)

"England were leading 3–2 and I fled into the next room, unable to watch. Suddenly, my father shouted, 'They've scored again!' Believing Germany had equalised once more I burst into tears . . ."

Former referee **David Elleray** recalling the 1966 World Cup final in *The Man in the Middle* (Time Warner Books, 2004)

"Sunday 14th June 1970: Tonight England was finally knocked out of the World Cup which, no doubt, will have another subtle effect on the public."

Labour Cabinet Minister **Tony Benn** writing during an election campaign which the Conservatives went on to win, *The Benn Diaries* (Hutchinson, 1995)

"The final whistle blew. We were in total despair. It was 3–2 to the Germans. We sat in front of the TV, numb. I thought Penny was getting the food together, so I went into the kitchen to see if I could help her. I knew she didn't mind watching football, and her favourite man was Bobby Charlton, but – and this really shook me – she was in floods of tears. What a girl."

Actor **Dennis Waterman** recalling England's exit from the 1970 World Cup. *ReMinder: My Autobiography* (Hutchinson, 2000)

"The penalties were missed and England were out. I finished the broadcast by saying, 'If you're going to have a few drinks tonight to drown your sorrows, do it safely, not aggressively. Be proud of England's performance in playing so well.'"

Des Lynam on England's 1990 World Cup exit, *I Should Have Been at Work!* (HarperCollins, 2003)

"The *Mirror*'s coverage of England's previous opponents in the tournament so far has grown increasingly hysterical and jingoistic. For Spain, we offered '10 Things You Didn't Know About the Spanish', the first being that they introduced syphilis to Britain."

Former *Mirror* editor **Piers Morgan** on Euro 96, *The Insider: The Private Diaries of a Scandalous Decade* (Ebury Press, 2005)

"The following Saturday, we beat Spain. The crowd were belting out the song again, all the flags were waving, the sun was shining, and I remember turning to Dave in what had become our regular spot in front of the press box, and saying, 'Have a good look at this, Dave. This is our perfect summer.'"

Comedian **Frank Skinner** on the Wembley crowd's response to his and David Baddiel's Euro 96 song 'Three Lions', *Frank Skinner* (Century, 2001)

"Right to the end it looked as though England would win; amazingly, they were a much better team than the other side even with David not there. But then they had the penalty shoot-out and two of them missed. England were out of the World Cup."

Victoria Beckham's analysis of England's 1998 World Cup defeat by Argentina, *Learning to Fly* (Michael Joseph, 2001)

— WORLD CUP FOOD HAMPER —

Concerned that his players would find the local Mexican grub far too spicy, Sir Alf Ramsey insisted that all England's food for the 1970 World Cup should be brought over from the UK. Shortly before the start of the tournament, a refrigerated container packed with familiar goodies was flown over by Findus, the squad's official food supplier. The contents included:

140 lbs of beefburgers
400 lbs of sausages
300 lbs frozen fish
Ten cases of tomato ketchup

— SIR ALF'S BARBED BON MOTS —

Sir Alf Ramsey's relations with the press were frosty at the best of times, but as a World Cup-winning manager the England boss was in a strong position to dish out some stick to the media pack. Here are some of his best lines to the press boys:

"What do you want me to do: write your column for you?"
(Replying to a reporter's question, 1963)

"Sorry, it's my day off."
(When approached for a short interview the day after England won the World Cup, 1966)

"You need me, I don't need you."
(To assembled journalists, 1967)

Reporter: "Hello, Sir Alf, do you remember me?"
Ramsey: "Yes, you're a pest."
(1970)

"I have to make a living just like you. I happen to make mine in a nice way. You make yours in a nasty way."
(1973)

— 1966: WHAT THE PAPERS SAID —

England's triumph at the 1966 World Cup was big news around the globe. Here's a small sample of the worldwide reaction:

"England were worthy winners, gaining their victory both convincingly and attractively."

Soviet Sports (USSR)

"The victory of the English, though their third goal may have aroused many doubts, was fair."

Diario de Noticias (Portugal)

"England's most glorious day – champions of the world. Uruguay was the only team the champions could not defeat. The masters of football are now undisputed."

El Pais (Spain)

"The English not only built up a superior volume of play, but showed greater staying power."

La Suisse (Switzerland)

"We hoped the best man would win and the best man did win."

L'Avennire d'Italia (Italy)

"England well deserved the World Cup. It was a triumph of strength and determination."

L'Humanite Dimanche (France)

— BOTTLE OF BEER KO'S BANKS —

England's chances of advancing to the semi-finals of the 1970 World Cup in Mexico were dealt a major blow when, two days before their quarter-final tie with West Germany, goalkeeper Gordon Banks went down with a stomach bug after drinking a bottle of beer. Conspiracy theorists have had a field day with this episode, suggesting that Banks was deliberately poisoned as part of a plot to prevent the World Cup holders from retaining the trophy. England manager Sir Alf Ramsey was among those who believed that Banks' illness was no accident. In 1994 he said: "I will swear, Banks was got at in some form or another, with drug or potion." Banks' recollections of the incident in his autobiography, meanwhile, provide as many questions as answers:

> "On the preceding Friday Alf [Ramsey] allowed us a beer with
> our evening meal. I can't remember if the bottle I was served
> was opened in my presence or not but I do know that half an
> hour after drinking it I felt very ill indeed."

Banks recovered sufficiently to pass a fitness test on the day of the
quarter-final and was named in the England side to face West
Germany. Just hours before the match he attended a team meeting in
Sir Alf Ramsey's hotel room:

> "As Alf began speaking I began groaning. The stomach cramps
> had returned with a vengeance . . . 'Well?' Alf enquired.
> I shook my head. 'Not well,' I replied."

Banks' place went to his deputy Peter Bonetti, who was at fault for
all three West German goals as England threw away a 2–0 lead to lose
their hold on the Jules Rimet trophy. Whether Banks' bottle of beer
had been deliberately tampered with or not there was no disputing
its profound impact on England's hopes of retaining the World Cup.

— ENGLAND AT THE EUROPEAN CHAMPIONSHIPS: 1996 —

The first major international tournament to be held in England since
the 1966 World Cup, the dramatic twists and turns of Euro 96
captivated the nation. The England team was centre stage throughout,
backed by a raucous, passionate Wembley crowd which adopted the
Skinner and Baddiel hit *Three Lions* as its new anthem.

Terry Venables' team, though, began disappointingly with a drab
1–1 draw in the opening game against Switzerland. The first half of
the derby with Scotland a week later was little better, but the game
came to life after the break. After Alan Shearer had headed England
in front, David Seaman brilliantly saved Gary McAllister's penalty
before, in the closing minutes, Paul Gascoigne scored a superb solo
goal to seal the home side's victory. England maintained their
momentum in the final group game, hammering Holland 4–1 in a
vibrant, attacking display which had Wembley in raptures.

The quarter-final against Spain was a tense, even affair which
eventually went to penalties. Again, Seaman was the hero, diving to
his left to save Nadal's spot-kick and book England a semi-final
meeting with Germany.

England got off to the best possible start when Shearer headed in
a flicked-on corner, but Germany soon equalised. The remainder of

the 90 minutes produced no more goals so the game moved on into extra time, with the outcome set to be decided by the first or 'golden' goal. Both teams came close to finding a winner, but not close enough – Gazza just failing to reach the ball with the goal gaping and Anderton hitting the post. Once more, penalties would have to settle the tie. With both sides' appointed five takers all hitting the target, the shoot-out moved into sudden death. Wembley held its collective breath as defender Gareth Southgate strode forward . . . and then let out a huge groan as his weak kick was easily saved by German goalkeeper Andreas Koepke. Seconds later Andreas Moller confidently lashed home the winning penalty for Germany, ensuring there would be no immediate end to the '30 years of hurt' England fans had been singing about all summer.

Group table

	P	W	D	L	F	A	Pts
England	3	2	1	0	7	2	7
Holland	3	1	1	1	3	4	4
Scotland	3	1	1	1	1	2	4
Switzerland	3	0	1	2	1	4	1

Date	Venue	Result
8th June 1996	Wembley	England 1 Switzerland 1
15th June 1996	Wembley	England 2 Scotland 0
18th June 1996	Wembley	England 4 Holland 1
22nd June 1996	Wembley	England 0 Spain 0*^
26th June 1996	Wembley	England 1 Germany 1*#

* after extra-time

^ England won 4–2 on penalties

Germany won 6–5 on penalties

England squad: Tony Adams (Arsenal, 5 apps), **Darren Anderton** (Tottenham, 5 apps), **Steve McManamam** (Liverpool, 5 apps), **Stuart Pearce** (Nottingham Forest, 5 apps), **David Seaman** (Arsenal, 5 apps), **Alan Shearer** (Blackburn, 5 apps), **Teddy Sheringham** (Tottenham, 5 apps), **Gareth Southgate** (Aston Villa, 5 apps), **Paul Ince** (Inter Milan, 4 apps), **Gary Neville** (Manchester United, 4 apps), **David Platt** (Arsenal, 2+2 apps), **Nick Barmby** (Middlesbrough, 0+3 apps), **Steve Stone** (Nottingham Forest, 0+3 apps), **Robbie Fowler** (Liverpool, 0+2 apps), **Sol Campbell** (Tottenham, 0+1 apps), **Jamie Redknapp** (Liverpool, 0+1 apps), **Les Ferdinand** (Newcastle United, 0 apps), **Tim Flowers** (Blackburn, 0 apps), **Steve Howey** (Newcastle United, 0 apps), **Phil Neville** (Manchester United, 0 apps), **Ian Walker** (Tottenham, 0 apps)

Goal scorers: Shearer 5, Sheringham 2, Gascoigne 1

Winners: Germany

They said it

"We can give a lot to people who are English, and who haven't felt too good about things for quite a few years."

Terry Venables, gets all philosophical before the semi-final with Germany

"Yet again we had been beaten on penalties. It all seemed so unfair. I was choked."

Paul Gascoigne

"I put the penalty where I wanted but not far enough in the corner. When he saved it, there was just an incredible sense of deflation, a sense of: this really wasn't meant to happen."

Gareth Southgate

Stuart Pearce after burying his demons in the shoot-out
v Spain at Euro 96

— ENGLAND V ARGENTINA: A 40-YEAR RIVALRY —

England and Argentina have fought some bitter battles over the years which together have contributed to one of the fiercest rivalries in world football:

1966: Argentina captain Antonio Rattin was sent off in the first half of the World Cup quarter-final between the teams for arguing with the referee but refused initially to leave the pitch. Play was held up for nine minutes while Rattin, surrounded by FIFA officials and policemen, demanded an interpreter. Following his departure the Argentinian approach, which had been extremely physical from the outset, became even more violent. "Never, in any other match, have I been kicked when the ball was at the other end," recalled England striker Roger Hunt. "I'd look round and one of their fellows would make a gesture of innocence. It was the worst behaviour I've ever experienced." When Geoff Hurst scored a late goal for England, thus avoiding the need for extra-time and the possible drawing of lots to decide a winner, Argentina's Oscar Mas punched a drunken spectator who ran on the pitch to celebrate. At the final whistle Alf Ramsey intervened to prevent his players swapping shirts with their opponents, and as the teams headed down the tunnel there was more pushing and shoving. After the match Ramsey described the Argentinians as 'animals', a comment he later retracted under pressure from the FA. The following day FIFA's disciplinary imposed the maximum possible fine on the Argentine FA, a paltry £85.

1977: On their first visit to Argentina since the controversial match at Wembley in 1966, England were greeted by a hostile crowd in Buenos Aires who chanted 'animales!' every time one of Don Revie's men touched the ball. A bad-tempered game deteriorated into outright violence in the last ten minutes when England midfielder Trevor Cherry was punched in the face by Bertoni and lost two of his teeth. Bizarrely, Cherry was shown the red card along with his attacker.

1986: With memories of the Falklands War still fresh, England and Argentina clashed again in the quarter-final of the World Cup in Mexico. Shortly after half-time Argentina captain Diego Maradona jumped for a high ball in England's penalty area and clearly punched the ball into the net with his hand. The England players were, naturally, outraged at this blatant piece of cheating. "No one could believe it," recalled goalkeeper Peter Shilton. "Everyone ran up to the referee, I ran up to him . . . it was just incredible that the goal was given. It's still hard to believe." Back in Argentina, however, Maradona's 'Hand of God' goal was celebrated as much as his brilliant second strike. "We blasted the English pirates with Maradona and a little hand," trumpeted Argentinian newspaper *Cronica*. "He who robs a thief has a thousand years of pardon."

1998: Once again the two sides met at the World Cup and once again the match was clouded in controversy. The key moment occurred just after half-time when David Beckham was fouled by Argentina's Diego Simeone. Despite having been warned by England manager Glenn Hoddle not to retaliate under any circumstances, Beckham reacted by flicking out a leg at Simeone and was promptly sent off by Danish referee Kim Nielsen. After their penalty shoot-out victory the Argentinians celebrated on their team bus by twirling their shirts above their heads – in full view of the dejected English players.

2002: Drawn in the same World Cup final group as Argentina, England exacted revenge for 1986 and 1998 with a 1–0 win over their arch enemies. Fittingly, it was David Beckham who scored the winning goal with a penalty after Michael Owen had been fouled in the box.

2005: England maintained the upper hand over Argentina with a thrilling 3–2 win in a friendly in Geneva, thanks to two late Michael Owen headers. Although the match itself was played in a good spirit, the bad blood between the sides was again in evidence when the South Americans arrived at the stadium on their team coach. Waving their shirts above their heads and leaping up and down, the Argentinians shouted 'Y ya lo ve, el que no salta es un ingles!' ('Let everybody see, whoever doesn't jump is an Englishman!') After the final whistle, in an echo of the notorious 1966 clash, the Argentinians refused to swap shirts with their opponents.

— TURKISH DELIGHT —

If you are an England goalkeeper the team you would most like to face surely has to be Turkey. In ten meetings with the Turks stretching back to 1984 England have not conceded a single goal, a phenomenal record given the huge strides Turkish football has made over the last twenty years – and all the more remarkable when you consider that minnows such as Luxembourg, Malta and San Marino have all managed at least one goal against England at some point.

The details of England's 10 consecutive clean sheets against Turkey are as follows:

Date	Venue	England goalkeeper	Result
14th Nov 1984	Istanbul	Peter Shilton	Turkey 0 England 4
16th Oct 1985	Wembley	Peter Shilton	England 5 Turkey 0
29th April 1987	Izmir	Chris Woods	Turkey 0 England 0
14th Oct 1987	Wembley	Peter Shilton	England 8 Turkey 0
1st May 1991	Izmir	David Seaman	Turkey 0 England 1
16th Oct 1991	Wembley	Chris Woods	England 1 Turkey 0
18th Nov 1992	Wembley	Chris Woods	England 4 Turkey 0
31st March 1993	Izmir	Chris Woods	Turkey 0 England 2
2nd April 2003	Stadium of Light	David James	England 2 Turkey 0
11th Oct 2003	Istanbul	David James	Turkey 0 England 0

— 'OH BOYO, ANYBODY BUT WALES' —

The late Emlyn Hughes represented England with distinction, making 62 appearances for his country between 1970 and 1980 and captaining the Three Lions on 23 occasions. Normally picked as a defender, Hughes only managed one goal for England, in a 3–0 victory against Wales at Ninian Park, Cardiff in May 1972. His father, Hughes later recalled, was less than delighted with his son's success:

> *"I saw my Dad in the car park afterwards and I thought I would get a hug and congratulations from him. I was his son and had just scored for England. Instead he bellowed: 'Oh, boyo, anybody else but Wales.'"*

— STAMP OF APPROVAL —

In 1996, Sir Bobby Charlton inadvertently became the first living person, other than a monarch, to appear on a British stamp. To mark the Euro 96 tournament in England, the Royal Mail produced a series featuring England internationals Dixie Dean (19p), Bobby Moore (25p) and Billy Wright (41p) and Irishman Danny Blanchflower (60p). The 35p stamp was captioned Duncan Edwards, but the picture was actually of a young Bobby Charlton, complete with a full head of hair.

— A GOAL . . . BUT STILL JUST ONE GAME —

You'd think that if you scored on your international debut you'd stand a more than reasonable chance of being called up for the next England game. Think again. These post-war players found the net when they first pulled on the Three Lions shirt but it was still a case of 'thank you, and goodbye' . . .

Player	Goal(s)	Date	Venue	Result
Jack Haines	2	1st December 1948	Highbury	England 6 Switzerland 0
Jackie Lee	1	7th October 1950	Belfast	N Ireland 1 England 4
Bill Nicholson	1	19th May 1951	Belfast	N Ireland 1 England 2
Geoff Bradford	1	2nd October 1955	Copenhagen	Denmark 1 England 5
Tony Kay	1	5th June 1963	Basle	Switzerland 1 England 8
Paul Goddard	1	2nd June 1982	Reykjavik	Iceland 1 England 1
Danny Wallace	1	29th January 1986	Cairo	Egypt 0 England 4
Francis Jeffers	1	12th February 2003	Upton Park	England 1 Australia 3

— STAN'S BAREFACED CHEEK —

In September 1947 England crossed the Channel to play a friendly against Belgium in Brussels. The match is remembered for an amusing incident involving Stanley Matthews, later recalled by England manager Walter Winterbottom:

> *"For entertainment and wizardry there was no-one better than Matthews. I'll never forget one match when we played Belgium. We were losing 2–1 at half-time. But the second half belonged to Stan. He took over and we won 5–2. The remainder of the goals were down to his extraordinary wizardry. One was amazing. He took off on one of his dribbles from the half-way line and the centre half, who was wearing gloves, dived at him*

to try and rugby tackle him to the ground. Instead, he pulled Stan's shorts down. Stan never flinched, went on with his mazy dribble even with his shorts around his knees. He ended the breathtaking run with a delicate chip for Tom Finney to score. Everyone in the ground rose to their feet, in stages, as the run went on. By the time the goal was scored, both sets of players were applauding Stan."

— ENGLAND AT THE EUROPEAN CHAMPIONSHIPS: 2000 —

Having stumbled through their qualification campaign, England were not especially fancied at the Euro 2000 finals in Holland and Belgium. Yet, after 20 minutes of their opening game against Portugal, Kevin Keegan's men looked like potential winners as they raced into a deserved two-goal lead. At the end of the 90 minutes, however, despair had replaced joy as the over-riding emotion after a stunning Figo strike and English defensive lapses combined to turn almost certain victory into a shattering defeat.

Five days later England produced a battling display to beat Germany 1–0, Alan Shearer's header deciding a scrappy contest in Charleroi. Needing just a draw against Romania to qualify for the quarter-finals England recovered from going a goal down to take a 2–1 lead, but were again undone by poor defensive play. First, Nigel Martyn failed to hold a cross, allowing Munteanu to level. Then, with just three minutes left on the clock, a rash challenge by Phil Neville resulted in Romania being awarded a penalty. Ioan Ganea scored to dump England out of the tournament at the first hurdle, a setback which raised probing questions about Keegan's style of management, his tactics and his future as England boss.

Group table

	P	W	D	L	F	A	Pts
Portugal	3	3	0	0	7	2	9
Romania	3	1	1	1	4	4	4
England	3	1	0	2	5	6	3
Germany	3	0	1	2	1	5	1

Date	Venue	Result
12th June 2000	Eindhoven	England 2 Portugal 3
17th June 2000	Charleroi	England 1 Germany 0
20th June 2000	Charleroi	England 2 Romania 3

England squad: David Beckham (Manchester United, 3 apps), **Sol Campbell** (Tottenham, 3 apps), **Paul Ince** (Middlesbrough, 3 apps), **Gary Neville** (Manchester United, 3 apps), **Phil Neville** (Manchester United, 3 apps), **Michael Owen** (Liverpool, 3 apps), **Paul Scholes** (Manchester United, 3 apps), **Alan Shearer** (Newcastle United, 3 apps), **Martin Keown** (Arsenal, 2+1 apps), **Dennis Wise** (Chelsea, 2+1 apps), **David Seaman** (Arsenal, 2 apps), **Tony Adams** (Arsenal, 1 app), **Steve McManaman** (Real Madrid, 1 app), **Nigel Martyn** (Leeds United, 1 app), **Nick Barmby** (Everton, 0+2 apps), **Emile Heskey** (Liverpool, 0+2 apps), **Steven Gerrard** (Liverpool, 0+1 apps), **Gareth Southgate** (Aston Villa, 0+1 apps), **Gareth Barry** (Aston Villa, 0 apps), **Robbie Fowler** (Liverpool, 0 apps), **Kevin Phillips** (Sunderland, 0 apps), **Richard Wright** (Ipswich, 0 apps)

Goal scorers: Shearer 2, McManaman 1, Owen 1, Scholes 1

Tournament winners: France

They said it

"I failed to get the best out of the players I chose and that is down to me. I wasn't able to get my team to do what I wanted them to do."
Kevin Keegan

"The bottom line is that we were inept tactically, we were exposed against teams we could have beaten. England's failings have nothing to do with technical skill because I don't agree we're not good enough as footballers."
Martin Keown

"Tony Blair is very good looking but unfortunately he has no bravado. Same with the England football team. They play so slow."
Adriana Sklenarikova, Slovakian Wonderbra model

— CALLY'S LONG WAIT REWARDED —

As a young Liverpool winger Ian Callaghan played twice for England in 1966, including the group game against France at the World Cup finals. However, for the next 11 years Cally found himself in international exile, despite winning a stack of medals with his club and being voted Footballer of the Year in 1974 by the Football Writers' Association. Finally, Callaghan was recalled to the England squad in 1977 by new boss Ron Greenwood and won two further caps for his country in games against Switzerland and Luxembourg. No other player – not even those whose careers were disrupted by the first or second world wars – has waited so long between England appearances.

— FOREIGN-SOUNDING XI —

Here's a team of England players who sound as though they should be lining up for the opposition rather than the Three Lions. But play for England they did – although in most cases they might just as easily have represented another country . . .

1. **Peter Bonetti** (7 caps, 1966–70, mother and father were both of Swiss parentage)
2. **Paul Konchesky** (2 caps, 2003– , name of Polish origin)
3. **Tony Dorigo** (15 caps, 1989–93, son of Italian immigrant to Australia)
4. **Pelham Von Donop** (2 caps, 1873–75, name of German origin)
5. **Mike Pejic** (4 caps, 1974, father born in Yugoslavia)
6. **Ugo Ehiogu** (4 caps, 1996–2002, family from Nigeria)
7. **John Salako** (5 caps, 1991, born in Nigeria)
8. **Colin Viljoen** (2 caps, 1975, naturalised South African)
9. **Percy Paravicini** (3 caps, 1883, name of Italian origin)
10. **Matthew Le Tissier** (8 caps, 1994–97, born in Guernsey)
11. **Graeme Le Saux** (36 caps, 1994–2000, born in Jersey)

— SEAMAN'S DODGY KIT —

David Seaman was one of England's best players at Euro 96, memorably saving penalties against Scotland and Spain as the Three Lions stormed to the semi-finals. While the critics lavished praise on the Arsenal goalie, they were less enamoured of his kit worn against Germany – an orange, yellow and green monstrosity that was likened by one pundit to 'a packet of Refreshers'. An earlier outfit had earned this response from *The Independent on Sunday:* "This spring David Seaman is wearing a banana yellow abattoir worker's smock with a fetching inlaid testcard motif, which is attractively repeated in a pair of radioactive side panels on his lycra-style shorts for that fire damaged tarpaulin look."

— BILLY'S SUNNY MISTAKE —

On 13th May 1949 England played Sweden at the Rasunda Stadium in Stockholm on a very sunny evening. England captain Billy Wright won the toss and elected to play into the dazzling sun in the first half, thinking it would be the same for the Swedes in the second. Sweden took a 3–0 lead at the break, but by the time the second half started the sun had gone down behind the stand! Sweden eventually won 3–1, their first ever victory over England.

— ENGLAND LEGENDS: BOBBY CHARLTON —

Playing alongside his brother Jack, Bobby Charlton was a key member of England's 1966 World Cup team. His contribution to the triumph was immense, and included some memorable highlights: notably, the weaving run and trademark thunderbolt shot which opened England's account against Mexico, and the two fine goals that saw off Portugal in the semi-final.

Although only 28, Charlton was an England veteran by 1966, having made his international debut in April 1958, just a couple of months after he survived the Munich air crash which killed eight of his Manchester United team-mates. At that stage of his career Charlton was an orthodox left-winger, but his exceptional control, impressive range of passing and, above all, his incredibly powerful shooting made him ideally suited to the attacking midfield role he was later allotted by England manager Alf Ramsey.

In April 1970 Charlton became only the second England player to win 100 caps, marking the occasion with a goal against Northern Ireland at Wembley. Later that year he travelled to his fourth World Cup, playing his last match for his country in the quarter-final defeat by West Germany in Mexico. Ramsey's decision to substitute Charlton during the match while England were leading 2–1 was widely criticised later, an indication of just how highly the midfielder was rated by his fellow countrymen. Knighted for his services to football in 1994, Sir Bobby is still England's highest ever scorer with 49 goals, although his record is likely to be broken in the next few years by Michael Owen. A true gentleman, you can bet that Charlton will be the first to congratulate Owen when that day arrives.

Bobby Charlton Factfile
Born: Ashington, 11th October 1937
Club: Manchester United
Caps: 106 (1958–70)
Goals: 49
England debut: Scotland 0 England 4, 19th April 1958
International honours: World Cup winner 1966, England captain 3 times (1969–70)

Others on Charlton

"He had gifts to die for. Wherever you went in the world the foreign football fans knew everything about Bobby Charlton. He was our Pele."
England team-mate **Alan Ball**

"Bobby deserves to keep the record. He was a much better player than me and scored far better goals."

Gary Lineker, after he retired from international football one goal short of Charlton's England record, 1992

The one and only Bobby Charlton

— THE HOME INTERNATIONAL CHAMPIONSHIP: THE END —

The annual Home International tournament was last competed for in 1983/84, 101 years after its creation. Although Wales and Northern Ireland were keen to continue the competition, England and Scotland announced that they were no longer prepared to participate. A number of factors led to the two nations pulling out: fixture congestion, declining attendances and, to a lesser extent, crowd problems at some of the matches.

Writing in the match programme for the final Home International against Northern Ireland, England manager Bobby Robson made clear his support for the FA's decision to abandon the competition: "I feel our players will be better served pitting their skills against continental opposition, rather than against those they meet week in, week out, during the season or, as often happens, against their very own club mates."

Bizarrely, the last Home International Championship in 1983/84 ended with all four teams level on three points each. Northern Ireland took the title on goal difference:

	P	W	D	L	F	A	Pts
Northern Ireland	3	1	1	1	3	2	3
Wales	3	1	1	1	3	3	3
England	3	1	1	1	2	2	3
Scotland	3	1	1	1	3	4	3

— WORLD CUP MARKSMEN —

Bobby Charlton may just have held off Gary Lineker in the all-time England goalscoring stakes, but the former Leicester, Barcelona and Tottenham striker has a clear lead over his rival when it comes to goals scored at the World Cup. Indeed, with ten goals to his name, Lineker is easily the most prolific Englishman at the finals:

Gary Lineker, 10 goals (1986–90)
Geoff Hurst, 5 goals (1966–70)
Bobby Charlton, 4 goals (1962–70)
Michael Owen, 4 goals (1998–2002)

— ENGLAND AT THE EUROPEAN CHAMPIONSHIPS: 2004 —

Following their decent showing at the 2002 World Cup and further strengthened by the emergence of young prodigy Wayne Rooney, England were among the favourites for the European championships in Portugal. The team lived up to their billing in the first match, taking the lead against reigning champions France before wasting a golden opportunity to double their advantage when David Beckham missed a penalty. The moment proved pivotal, as France responded with two late goals by Zinedine Zidane to take the points.

A routine win over a mediocre Swiss side put England back on course, setting up a crunch meeting with Croatia in the final group game. Eriksson's men survived the shock of going a goal down to win 4–2, Rooney scoring twice in a bravura performance. England's failure to win the group, however, brought a heavy price: a decidedly tricky quarter-final with the hosts in their Lisbon stronghold.

An early goal by Michael Owen, the former teen hero now largely overshadowed by his new strike partner, gave England the best possible start. Minutes later, however, disaster struck when Rooney hobbled off with a broken foot. Lacking their star attacker, England retreated into a defensive shell which was eventually breached six minutes from time by Postiga's header. Right on full time Sol Campbell thought he'd put England through to the semi-finals but his header was ruled out by Swiss referee Urs Meier for an innocuous push on the Portuguese keeper. Portugal took the lead in extra-time only for Frank Lampard to pop up with his third and most vital goal of the tournament.

So yet again, England's hopes of success at a major tournament depended on the result of a penalty shoot-out . . . and, yet again, those hopes were extinguished as first Beckham and then Rooney's replacement, Darius Vassell, failed to convert from the spot. Not for the first time, the football gods had conspired to deny England in the most heartbreaking manner imaginable.

Group table

	P	W	D	L	F	A	Pts
France	3	2	1	0	7	4	7
England	3	2	0	1	8	4	6
Croatia	3	0	2	1	4	6	2
Switzerland	3	0	1	2	2	6	1

Date	Venue	Result
13th June 2004	Lisbon	England 1 France 2
17th June 2004	Coimbra	England 3 Switzerland 0
21st June 2004	Lisbon	England 4 Croatia 2
24th June 2004	Lisbon	Portugal 2 England 2*^

* after extra time

^ Portugal won 6–5 on penalties

England squad: David Beckham (Real Madrid, 4 apps), **Sol Campbell** (Arsenal, 4 apps), **Ashley Cole** (Arsenal, 4 apps), **Steven Gerrard** (Liverpool, 4 apps), **David James** (Manchester City, 4 apps), **Frank Lampard** (Chelsea, 4 apps), **Gary Neville** (Manchester United, 4 apps), **Michael Owen** (Liverpool, 4 apps), **Wayne Rooney** (Everton, 4 apps), **Paul Scholes** (Manchester United, 4 apps), **John Terry** (Chelsea, 3 apps), **Ledley King** (Tottenham, 1+1 apps), **Darius Vassell** (Aston Villa, 0+4 apps), **Owen Hargreaves** (Bayern Munich, 0+3 apps), **Phil Neville** (Manchester United, 0+2 apps), **Kieron Dyer** (Newcastle United, 0+1 apps), **Emile Heskey** (Birmingham City, 0+1 apps), **Wayne Bridge** (Chelsea, 0 apps), **Nicky Butt** (Manchester United, 0 apps), **Jamie Carragher** (Liverpool, 0 apps), **Joe Cole** (Chelsea, 0 apps), **Paul Robinson** (Tottenham, 0 apps), **Ian Walker** (Leicester City, 0 apps)

Goal scorers: Rooney 4, Lampard 3, Gerrard 1, Owen 1, Scholes 1

Tournament winners: Greece

They said it

"I don't remember anyone making such an impact on a tournament since Pele in the 1958 World Cup."

Sven-Goran Eriksson lavishes praise on Wayne Rooney

"We had a goal at full time that was basically a fair goal taken away. There was nothing wrong with it."

Frank Lampard, putting England's elimination down to the referee

"It's a big disappointment; to be fair to them they put their penalties away really well."

Michael Owen, generous in defeat after the Portugal match

— ENGLAND LEGENDS: PAUL GASCOIGNE —

One of the most naturally gifted players ever to play for his country, Paul Gascoigne shot to stardom in the 1990 World Cup when his dynamic performances in midfield for England helped propel Bobby Robson's side to a semi-final meeting with West Germany. However, a superb display in that game was overshadowed by a reckless tackle which earned him a booking and a suspension for the next match. Distraught at the prospect of missing the final, Gazza promptly burst into tears – a response which epitomised his endearing, but somewhat childlike and immature, personality.

For a brief period, 'Gazza-mania' swept the country, but a bad knee injury sustained in the 1991 FA Cup final reduced his impact over the following years. Gascoigne's lifestyle was also a cause of concern to his managers, leading England boss Graham Taylor to publicly question the player's 'refuelling habits' – a coded reference to Gazza's heavy drinking.

At Euro 96, however, the enigmatic Geordie was back to his best, using his deft ball control to sidestep opponents and setting up chances for his team-mates with cleverly angled passes. Most memorably, he also scored the goal of the tournament, cheekily flicking the ball over the head of Scotland defender Colin Hendry before sending a crashing volley into the corner of the net.

Gascoigne was again inspirational as England won a vital point in Rome to qualify for the 1998 World Cup. However, as the start of the tournament approached Gazza's form and fitness dipped, amid some sensational tabloid headlines about his off-the-pitch antics. To Gascoigne's dismay, Glenn Hoddle decided to leave him out of the World Cup squad, bringing down the curtain on a colourful and eventful England career.

Paul Gascoigne Factfile
Born: Gateshead, 25th May 1967
Clubs: Tottenham, Lazio, Rangers, Middlesbrough, Everton, Burton Albion
Caps: 57 (1988–98)
Goals: 10
England debut: England 1 Denmark 0, 14th September 1988 (sub)

Others on Gascoigne

"The bigger the game, the more Paul loved it. In England colours, he was like a dog with a bone."

Sir Bobby Robson

"All the time I was in the squad, it was Gazza who provided the light relief. He was also the best footballer, a genuine match winner. When he was flying, he was world class."

England team-mate **Stuart Pearce**

Gazza's tears in 1990

— WHICH SIDE ARE YOU ON? —

Since the early 1960s FIFA has prohibited players from appearing for more than one national team. However, before then it was not unknown for a player to turn out for two or, in the case of Real Madrid star Alfredo di Stefano, three different countries (Argentina, Colombia and Spain).

In the years before the one-country rule was introduced four England internationals also played for another national team:

Jack Reynolds

Born in Blackburn in 1869, Reynolds moved to Ireland as a boy. He made five appearances for Ireland while playing for Distillery and Ulster, scoring a goal against England in his side's 9–1 defeat in Belfast in 1890. After moving to England to play for West Bromwich Albion Reynolds won eight caps at half-back for his birth nation between 1892 and 1897. He is the only player to have scored for and against England.

John Edwards

Born in Shrewsbury in 1850, Edwards made one appearance for England against Scotland in 1874 while playing for Shropshire Wanderers. In 1876 he became the first treasurer of the Football Association of Wales and, later the same year, played for his adopted country in their first ever international, a 4–0 defeat against Scotland in Glasgow.

Bobby Evans

The son of Welsh parents, Evans was born in Chester in 1885. He was a regular for Wales between 1906 and 1910, winning 10 caps. When the England selectors discovered the Sheffield United player had been born in Cheshire, Evans was called up for international duty by his birth nation. He won four caps for England between 1911 and 1912.

Ken Armstrong

A member of Chelsea's 1955 title-winning side, Bradford-born Armstrong was capped by England in the 7–2 rout of Scotland that same year. In 1957 he emigrated to New Zealand and made 13 appearances for the Kiwis between 1958 and 1964, while also serving as the chief coach of the New Zealand FA.

— SVEN-GORAN ERIKSSON'S FIRST ENGLAND TEAM —

The appointment of Swedish coach Sven Goran-Eriksson as England's first foreign manager in January 2001 was not greeted with universal approval in the wider football community. Reaction to the news was particularly hostile in the tabloid newspapers, who felt that the national team should be managed by a born-and-bred Englishman. In *The Daily Mail*, for instance, veteran sports reporter Jeff Powell claimed, "We've sold our birthright down the fjord to a nation of seven million skiers and hammer throwers who spend half their lives in darkness."

Not that the furore surrounding his appointment cut any ice with the apparently unflappable Eriksson, who simply went about his business watching as many Premiership players as possible before his first game in charge against Spain at Villa Park in February 2001. The team he chose for the match included one major surprise in the form of left-back debutante Chris Powell, while his use of a large number of substitutes – in this case seven – was to become something of an Eriksson trademark in the coming years . . .

1. **David James** (Aston Villa)
2. **Phil Neville** (Manchester United)
3. **Chris Powell** (Charlton)
4. **Nicky Butt** (Manchester United)
5. **Rio Ferdinand** (Leeds United)
6. **Sol Campbell** (Tottenham)
7. **David Beckham** (Manchester United, captain)
8. **Paul Scholes** (Manchester United)
9. **Andy Cole** (Manchester United)
10. **Michael Owen** (Liverpool)
11. **Nick Barmby** (Liverpool)

Substitutes: **Michael Ball** (Everton), **Ugo Ehiogu** (Middlesbrough), **Emile Heskey** (Liverpool), **Frank Lampard jnr** (West Ham United), **Nigel Martyn** (Leeds United), **Gavin McCann** (Sunderland), **Gary Neville** (Manchester United)

— FIVE MINUTES OF FAME —

The shortest recorded England career is that of Brighton striker Peter Ward, whose sole appearance for his country consisted of a five-minute run-out as sub against Australia in Sydney on 31st May 1980. Ward beat a record previously held by 15-stone Jimmy Barrett of West Ham, whose one appearance for England against Northern Ireland at Goodison Park in October 1928 was abruptly ended by injury after just eight minutes.

— THE NEW WEMBLEY —

The new Wembley Stadium, designed by the architects Foster and Partners, boasts a number of eye-catching features:

- A 133-metre tall arch which is visible right across London. The arch supports the north stand and much of the south stand, and at 315 metres in length is the longest single span roof structure in the world.
- A sliding 52-metre tall roof, which will be left open between events allowing air to circulate over the pitch, but which can be moved to line up with the touchlines in just 15 minutes, ensuring that every spectator is sheltered during a match.
- 90,000 seats, all with an unobstructed view. Every seat will have more leg room than those in the Royal Box at the old Wembley.
- A 20 ft bronze statue of England World Cup-winning captain Bobby Moore by sculptor Philip Jackson, standing outside the main entrance.

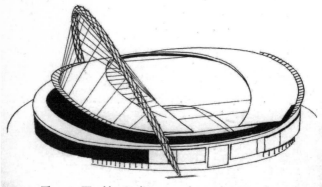

The new Wembley Stadium: complete with 2,618 toilets!

- 2,618 toilets, a figure unsurpassed by any other building in the world.
- A Royal Box in the same position as the one in the old Wembley, in the middle of the north stand.
- Two giant television screens, each the size of 600 domestic TV screens.
- A temporary athletics platform that can be installed when necessary. The platform will cover some of the seats but create the extra space needed to fit an athletics track.
- The total cost of the stadium, £352 million (or £3,918 per seat), makes it the most expensive in the world to date.

— ENGLAND'S FIRST EVER PENALTY —

England's first ever penalty was awarded in a match against Ireland at Sunderland on 18th February 1899, some eight years after penalties were introduced to the game. Jimmy Crabtree of Aston Villa took the kick and, a portent of years of agony to come, perhaps, he missed. It hardly mattered, though, as England still won 13–2. Although had he scored, England would have beaten their (still existing) record score, 13–0 against Ireland in 1882.

— AN ICONIC BALL —

Despite scoring a hat-trick in the 1966 World Cup final Geoff Hurst did not take home the match ball. Instead, it was nabbed by West Germany's Helmut Haller who claimed the ball according to the German custom that the first goalscorer in a final is entitled to keep it.

Shortly before the start of Euro 96 two British tabloid newspapers, *The Sun* and *The Daily Mirror* both decided that it was time to return the talismanic object to its rightful owner. The rival teams of reporters eventually tracked Haller down to a sports shop in Augsberg and the dusty old amber ball was retrieved from a cellar in his son's home near Munich. After lengthy negotiations, Haller agreed to part with it for £80,000, with the proceeds going to charity.

The Daily Mirror won the race to reclaim the stolen icon for Hurst, and in the following day's paper the former England striker was quoted as saying, "It's a piece of our history. I never thought I'd see it again." The ball is now on display in the National Football Museum in Preston.

— DON'T QUOTE ME 3 —

"That man could talk and talk and talk until the cows came home and he'd continue talking until they were fast asleep. The problem was most of it didn't make any sense to me."

Ian Wright on Graham Taylor's England team talks

"If Glenn Hoddle said one word to his team at half-time, it was concentration and focus."

Ron Atkinson, commentating on England-Argentina, 1998

"In the studio, Des Lynam's line-up of pundits resembled an evolutionary wall-chart of human articulacy, starting with Paul Gascoigne at the primeval end and peaking, surprisingly, with Gary Neville."

Mail on Sunday TV critic **David Bennun** on ITV's coverage of England-Denmark, 2002

"At Wembley it got warmer and warmer as you went up the tunnel and what hit you, apart from the noise, was the smell of fried onions."

England striker **Malcolm MacDonald** recalls the old Wembley atmosphere,

"I'm the man for the job. I can revive our World Cup hopes. I couldn't do a worse job, could I?"

Monster Raving Loony Party leader **Screaming Lord Sutch** puts his name in the frame for the England job, 1994

"I read it in the papers every World Cup that this will be England's year. They won't win, just like Tim Henman never wins the Wimbledon title."

George Best, 2005

— FIRST AMONG EQUALS —

The Football Writers' Player of the Year award has been awarded since 1948 to the most outstanding footballer of the season. Although achievements in domestic football count for much, feats on the international stage are also taken into consideration by the voters. The England internationals to have won this prestigious award are:

1948 Stanley Matthews	1974 Ian Callaghan
1950 Joe Mercer	1975 Alan Mullery
1951 Harry Johnston	1976 Kevin Keegan
1952 Billy Wright	1977 Emlyn Hughes
1953 Nat Lofthouse	1980 Terry McDermott
1954 Tom Finney	1982 Steve Perryman
1955 Don Revie	1986 Gary Lineker
1957 Tom Finney	1987 Clive Allen
1959 Syd Owen	1988 John Barnes
1960 Bill Slater	1990 John Barnes
1963 Stanley Matthews	1992 Gary Lineker
1964 Bobby Moore	1993 Chris Waddle
1966 Bobby Charlton	1994 Alan Shearer
1967 Jack Charlton	2001 Teddy Sheringham
1972 Gordon Banks	2005 Frank Lampard

— CURTAILED NAME XI —

Not much money to be made here for the replica shirt salesmen . . . a team of England internationals comprised entirely of players with just three letters in their surname:

1. **Freddie Fox** (1 cap, 1925)
2. **C.B. Fry** (1 cap, 1901)
3. **Bernard Joy** (1 cap, 1938)
4. **Rob Lee** (21 caps, 1994–98)
5. **Tony Kay** (1 cap, 1963)
6. **Charles Gee** (3 caps, 1931–36)
7. **Ronald Dix** (1 cap, 1938)
8. **Samuel Day** (3 caps, 1906)
9. **Jesse Pye** (1 cap, 1949)
10. **John Cox** (3 caps, 1901–03)
11. **Graham Rix** (17 caps, 1980–84)

— IN GOOD COMPANY —

England's leading scorer at the World Cup, Gary Lineker, is currently ranked joint fifth in the list of all-time top scorers at the tournament:

Position	Player	Goals	Years
1st	Gerd Muller (West Germany)	14	1970, 1974
2nd	Just Fontaine (France)	13	1958
3rd	Pele (Brazil)	12	1958, 1962, 1966, 1970
	Ronaldo (Brazil)	12	1994, 1998, 2002
4th	Sandor Kocsis (Hungary)	11	1954
	Jurgen Klinsmann (Germany)	11	1990, 1994
5th	Helmut Rahn (West Germany)	10	1954
	Teofilo Cubillas (Peru)	10	1970, 1978
	Gregorz Lato (Poland)	10	1974, 1978, 1982
	Gary Lineker (England)	**10**	**1986, 1990**
	Gabriel Batistuta (Argentina)	10	1994, 1998, 2002

— ENGLAND 9 SCOTLAND 3 —

On 15th April 1961 England ran up this cricket score (well, OK, rugby score) against Scotland at Wembley – their biggest ever win in the world's oldest international fixture. In goal for the Scots was Celtic keeper Frank Haffey and the following day's newspapers revelled in his misery, with one headline reading 'What's the score? Nine past Haffey!'

The England scorers at Wembley were:
Jimmy Greaves, 3
Bobby Smith, 2
Johnny Haynes, 2
Bryan Douglas, 1
Bobby Robson, 1

Even to this day the Scots hate to be reminded about this national humiliation. "In Scotland they try to erase the game from the memory," observed Jimmy Armfield, who played for England in the match. "If you tried to talk about it they'd change the subject."

— ENGLAND V THE REST —

On three occasions England have played full internationals against pick 'n' mix selections of the best players in the world. The details of these games are as follows:

Date	Venue	Result
26th Oct 1938	Highbury	England 3 Rest of Europe 0
21st Oct 1953	Wembley	England 4 Rest of Europe 4
23rd Oct 1963	Wembley	England 2 Rest of World 1

The 1963 Rest of The World team was an especially glittering selection, including such names as Spain's Alfredo di Stefano, Hungarian legend Ferenc Puskas, Russian goalkeeper Lev Yashin and Portuguese star Eusebio. Two Scots, Jim Baxter and Denis Law, also made the squad.

— ONE-CAP WONDER XI —

A team of players who appeared just the once for England:

1. **Alex Stepney** (Manchester United, v Sweden 1968)
2. **Bill Nicholson** (Tottenham, v Portugal 1951)
3. **Mel Sterland** (Sheffield Wednesday, v Saudi Arabia 1988)
4. **John Hollins** (Chelsea, v Spain 1967)
5. **Jeff Blockley** (Arsenal, v Yugoslavia 1972)
6. **Tommy Smith** (Liverpool, v Wales 1971)
7. **Mark Walters** (Rangers, v New Zealand 1991)
8. **Lee Bowyer** (Leeds, v Portugal 2003)
9. **John Richards** (Wolves, v Northern Ireland 1973)
10. **Charlie George** (Derby County, v Republic of Ireland 1976)
11. **Alan Thompson** (Celtic, v Sweden 2004)

— '66 HEROES IN THE DUGOUT —

Despite being members of the greatest ever England team, apart from Jack Charlton with the Republic of Ireland the World Cup winners of 1966 made little impression in management. The league clubs they managed were:

Manager	Club	Trophies
Alan Ball	Blackpool (1980–81)	–
	Portsmouth (1984–89 and 1998–99)	–
	Southampton (1994–95)	–
	Manchester City (1995–96)	–

Bobby Charlton	Preston (1973–75)	–
Jack Charlton	Middlesbrough (1973–77)	Div 2 title (1974)
	Sheffield Wednesday (1977–83)	–
	Newcastle United (1984–85)	–
Geoff Hurst	Chelsea (1979–81)	–
Bobby Moore	Southend United (1984–86)	–
Martin Peters	Sheffield United (1981)	–
Nobby Stiles	Preston (1977–81)	–

— CLEAN SHEETS ALL ROUND —

Remarkably, England qualified for the 1990 World Cup in Italy without conceding a single goal in six group matches. Peter Shilton, England's most-capped player, was in goal for all six games.

Date	Venue	Result
19th Oct 1988	Wembley	England 0 Sweden 0
8th Mar 1989	Tirana	Albania 0 England 2
26th April 1989	Wembley	England 5 Albania 0
3rd June 1989	Wembley	England 3 Poland 0
6th Sept 1989	Stockholm	Sweden 0 England 0
11th Oct 1989	Katowice	Poland 0 England 0

— BAD BOYS —

England players receiving more than one World Cup caution:

Terry Fenwick, 3 (1986)
Ray Wilkins, 3* (1982–86)
Terry Butcher, 2 (1982–86)
Sol Campbell, 2 (1998–2002)
Paul Gascoigne, 2 (1990)
Francis Lee, 2 (1970)
Paul Scholes, 2 (1998–2002)
* Including two in the same match v Morocco in 1986, leading to a red card

Among the 18 England players to receive one yellow card at the World Cup is the squeaky-clean figure of Bobby Charlton, whose caution for dissent against Argentina at the 1966 tournament was the only yellow card of his 106-cap international career.

— A JOB LOT OF SMITHS —

Predictably, perhaps, more players called 'Smith' have represented England than players with any other surname – 20 at the last count. All rather confusing, we think you'll agree, but perhaps less so after you've studied this definitive list of England 'Smudgers':

Player	Club	Position	Caps
Alan Smith	Arsenal	Striker	13 (1988–92)
Alan Smith	Leeds/Man Utd	Striker	16 (2001–)
Albert Smith	Nottingham Forest	Right-half	3 (1891–93)
Arnold Smith	Oxford University	Forward	1 (1872)
Bert Smith	Tottenham	Right-half	2 (1921–22)
Bobby Smith	Tottenham	Centre forward	15 (1960–63)
Charles Smith	Crystal Palace	Forward	1 (1876)
Gilbert Smith	Oxford University, Old Carthusians, Corinthians	Centre forward	20 (1893–1901)
Herbert Smith	Reading	Left-back	4 (1905–06)
James Smith	Millwall	Outside-left	2 (1938)
John Smith	Portsmouth	Inside-right	3 (1931)
Joe Smith	Bolton	Inside-left	5 (1913–20)
Joseph Smith	WBA	Right-back	2 (1919–22)
Leslie Smith	Brentford	Outside-left	1 (1939)
Lionel Smith	Arsenal	Left-back	6 (1950–53)
Sep Smith	Leicester City	Right-half	1 (1935)
Stephen Smith	Aston Villa	Outside-left	1 (1895)
Tommy Smith	Liverpool	Midfielder	1 (1971)
Trevor Smith	Birmingham City	Centre-half	2 (1959)
William Smith	Huddersfield Town	Outside-left	3 (1922–28)

— ENGLAND'S RESULTS 1872–2005 —

Key

WC	World Cup	Fr	Friendly
WCq	World Cup qualifier	(H)	Home
EC	European Championship	(A)	Away
ECq	European Championship qualifier	(N)	Neutral
HC	Home Championship	*	After extra-time
RC	Rous Cup	+	Won on penalties
T	Other tournament	^	Lost on penalties

Year	Opponent	Competition	Result
1872	Scotland	Fr	(A) 0–0
1873	Scotland	Fr	(H) 4–2
1874	Scotland	Fr	(A) 1–2
1875	Scotland	Fr	(H) 2–2
1876	Scotland	Fr	(A) 0–3
1877	Scotland	Fr	(H) 1–3
1878	Scotland	Fr	(A) 2–7
1879	Wales	Fr	(H) 2–1
	Scotland	Fr	(H) 5–4
1880	Scotland	Fr	(A) 4–5
	Wales	Fr	(A) 3–2
1881	Wales	Fr	(H) 0–1
	Scotland	Fr	(H) 1–6
1882	Ireland	Fr	(A) 13–0
	Scotland	Fr	(A) 1–5
	Wales	Fr	(A) 3–5
1883	Wales	Fr	(H) 5–0
	Ireland	Fr	(H) 7–0
	Scotland	Fr	(H) 2–3
1884	Ireland	HC	(A) 8–1
	Scotland	HC	(A) 0–1
	Wales	HC	(H) 4–0
1885	Ireland	HC	(H) 4–0
	Wales	HC	(H) 1–1
	Scotland	HC	(H) 1–1
1886	Ireland	HC	(A) 6–1
	Wales	HC	(A) 3–1
	Scotland	HC	(A) 1–1
1887	Ireland	HC	(H) 7–0
	Wales	HC	(H) 4–0
	Scotland	HC	(H) 2–3
1888	Wales	HC	(H) 5–1
	Scotland	HC	(A) 5–0
	Ireland	HC	(A) 5–1
1889	Wales	HC	(H) 4–1
	Ireland	HC	(H) 6–1
	Scotland	HC	(H) 2–3
1890	Ireland	HC	(A) 9–1
	Wales	HC	(A) 3–1

	Scotland	HC	(A)	1–1
1891	Wales	HC	(H)	4–1
	Ireland	HC	(H)	6–1
	Scotland	HC	(H)	2–1
1892	Wales	HC	(A)	2–0
	Ireland	HC	(A)	2–0
	Scotland	HC	(A)	4–1
1893	Ireland	HC	(H)	6–1
	Wales	HC	(H)	6–0
	Scotland	HC	(H)	5–2
1894	Ireland	HC	(A)	2–2
	Wales	HC	(A)	5–1
	Scotland	HC	(A)	2–2
1895	Ireland	HC	(H)	9–0
	Wales	HC	(H)	1–1
	Scotland	HC	(H)	3–0
1896	Ireland	HC	(A)	2–0
	Wales	HC	(A)	9–1
	Scotland	HC	(A)	1–2
1897	Ireland	HC	(H)	6–0
	Wales	HC	(H)	4–0
	Scotland	HC	(H)	1–2
1898	Ireland	HC	(A)	3–2
	Wales	HC	(A)	3–0
	Scotland	HC	(A)	3–1
1899	Ireland	HC	(H)	13–2
	Wales	HC	(H)	4–1
	Scotland	HC	(H)	2–1
1900	Ireland	HC	(A)	2–0
	Wales	HC	(A)	1–1
	Scotland	HC	(A)	1–4
1901	Ireland	HC	(H)	3–0
	Wales	HC	(H)	6–0
	Scotland	HC	(H)	2–2
1902	Wales	HC	(A)	0–0
	Ireland	HC	(A)	1–0
	Scotland	HC	(H)	2–2
1903	Ireland	HC	(H)	4–0
	Wales	HC	(H)	2–1
	Scotland	HC	(H)	1–2
1904	Wales	HC	(A)	2–2
	Ireland	HC	(A)	3–1
	Scotland	HC	(A)	1–0
1905	Ireland	HC	(H)	1–1
	Wales	HC	(H)	3–0
	Scotland	HC	(H)	1–0
1906	Ireland	HC	(A)	5–0
	Wales	HC	(A)	1–0
	Scotland	HC	(A)	1–2
1907	Ireland	HC	(H)	1–0
	Wales	HC	(H)	1–1
	Scotland	HC	(H)	1–1
1908	Ireland	HC	(A)	3–1

	Wales	HC	(A)	7–1
	Scotland	HC	(A)	1–1
	Austria	Fr	(A)	6–1
	Austria	Fr	(A)	11–1
	Hungary	Fr	(A)	7–0
	Bohemia	Fr	(A)	4–0
1909	Ireland	HC	(H)	4–0
	Wales	HC	(H)	2–0
	Scotland	HC	(H)	2–0
	Hungary	Fr	(A)	4–2
	Hungary	Fr	(A)	8–2
	Austria	Fr	(A)	8–1
1910	Ireland	HC	(A)	1–1
	Wales	HC	(A)	1–0
	Scotland	HC	(A)	0–2
1911	Ireland	HC	(H)	2–1
	Wales	HC	(H)	3–0
	Scotland	HC	(H)	1–1
1912	Ireland	HC	(A)	6–1
	Wales	HC	(A)	2–0
	Scotland	HC	(A)	1–1
1913	Ireland	HC	(A)	1–2
	Wales	HC	(H)	4–3
	Scotland	HC	(H)	1–0
1914	Ireland	HC	(H)	0–3
	Wales	HC	(A)	2–0
	Scotland	HC	(A)	1–3
1919	Ireland	HC	(A)	1–1
1920	Wales	HC	(H)	1–2
	Scotland	HC	(H)	5–4
	Ireland	HC	(H)	2–0
1921	Wales	HC	(A)	0–0
	Scotland	HC	(A)	0–3
	Belgium	Fr	(A)	2–0
	N Ireland	HC	(A)	1–1
1922	Wales	HC	(H)	1–0
	Scotland	HC	(H)	0–1
	N Ireland	HC	(H)	2–0
1923	Wales	HC	(A)	2–2
	Belgium	Fr	(H)	6–1
	Scotland	HC	(A)	2–2
	France	Fr	(A)	4–2
	Sweden	Fr	(A)	4–2
	Sweden	Fr	(A)	3–1
	N Ireland	HC	(A)	1–2
	Belgium	Fr	(A)	2–2
1924	Wales	HC	(H)	1–2
	Scotland	HC	(H)	1–1
	France	Fr	(A)	3–1
	N Ireland	HC	(H)	3–1
	Belgium	Fr	(H)	4–0
1925	Wales	HC	(A)	2–1
	Scotland	HC	(A)	0–2

	France	Fr	(A) 3–2
	N Ireland	HC	(A) 0–0
1926	Wales	HC	(H) 1–3
	Scotland	HC	(H) 1–0
	Belgium	Fr	(A) 5–3
	N Ireland	HC	(H) 3–3
1927	Wales	HC	(A) 3–3
	Scotland	HC	(A) 2–1
	Belgium	Fr	(A) 9–1
	Luxembourg	Fr	(A) 5–2
	France	Fr	(A) 6–0
	N Ireland	HC	(A) 0–2
	Wales	HC	(H) 1–2
1928	Scotland	HC	(H) 1–5
	France	Fr	(A) 5–1
	Belgium	Fr	(A) 3–1
	N Ireland	HC	(H) 2–1
	Wales	HC	(A) 3–2
1929	Scotland	HC	(A) 0–1
	France	Fr	(A) 4–1
	Belgium	Fr	(A) 5–1
	Spain	Fr	(A) 3–4
	N Ireland	HC	(A) 3–0
	Wales	HC	(H) 6–0
1930	Scotland	HC	(H) 5–2
	Germany	Fr	(A) 3–3
	Austria	Fr	(A) 0–0
	N Ireland	HC	(H) 5–1
	Wales	HC	(A) 4–0
1931	Scotland	HC	(A) 0–2
	France	Fr	(A) 2–5
	Belgium	Fr	(A) 4–1
	N Ireland	HC	(A) 6–2
	Wales	HC	(H) 3–1
	Spain	Fr	(A) 7–1
1932	Scotland	HC	(H) 3–0
	N Ireland	HC	(H) 1–0
	Wales	HC	(A) 0–0
	Austria	Fr	(H) 4–3
1933	Scotland	HC	(A) 1–2
	Italy	Fr	(A) 1–1
	Switzerland	Fr	(A) 4–0
	N Ireland	HC	(A) 3–0
	Wales	HC	(H) 1–2
	France	Fr	(H) 4–1
1934	Scotland	HC	(H) 3–0
	Hungary	Fr	(A) 1–2
	Czechoslovakia	Fr	(A) 1–2
	Wales	HC	(A) 4–0
	Italy	Fr	(H) 3–2
1935	N Ireland	HC	(H) 2–1
	Scotland	HC	(A) 0–2
	Holland	Fr	(A) 1–0

	N Ireland	HC	(A) 3–1
	Germany	Fr	(H) 3–0
1936	Wales	HC	(H) 1–2
	Scotland	HC	(H) 1–1
	Austria	Fr	(A) 1–2
	Belgium	Fr	(A) 2–3
	Wales	HC	(A) 1–2
	N Ireland	HC	(H) 3–1
	Hungary	Fr	(H) 6–2
1937	Scotland	HC	(A) 1–3
	Norway	Fr	(A) 6–0
	Sweden	Fr	(A) 4–0
	Finland	Fr	(A) 8–0
	N Ireland	HC	(A) 5–1
	Wales	HC	(H) 2–1
	Czechoslovakia	Fr	(H) 5–4
1938	Scotland	HC	(H) 0–1
	Germany	Fr	(A) 6–3
	Switzerland	Fr	(A) 1–2
	France	Fr	(A) 4–2
	Wales	HC	(A) 2–4
	Rest of Europe	Fr	(H) 3–0
	Norway	Fr	(H) 4–0
	N Ireland	HC	(H) 7–0
1939	Scotland	HC	(A) 2–1
	Italy	Fr	(A) 2–1
	Yugoslavia	Fr	(A) 1–1
	Romania	Fr	(A) 2–0
1946	N Ireland	HC	(A) 7–2
	Republic Ireland	Fr	(A) 1–0
	Wales	HC	(H) 3–0
	Holland	Fr	(H) 8–2
1947	Scotland	HC	(H) 1–1
	France	Fr	(H) 3–0
	Switzerland	Fr	(A) 0–1
	Portugal	Fr	(A) 10–0
	Belgium	Fr	(A) 5–2
	Wales	HC	(A) 3–0
	N Ireland	HC	(H) 2–2
	Sweden	Fr	(H) 4–2
1948	Scotland	HC	(A) 2–0
	Italy	Fr	(A) 4–0
	Denmark	Fr	(A) 0–0
	N Ireland	HC	(A) 6–2
	Wales	HC	(H) 1–0
	Switzerland	Fr	(H) 6–0
1949	Scotland	HC	(H) 1–3
	Sweden	Fr	(A) 1–3
	Norway	Fr	(A) 4–1
	France	Fr	(A) 3–1
	Republic Ireland	Fr	(H) 0–2
	Wales	HC/WCq	(A) 4–1
	N Ireland	HC/WCq	(H) 9–2

	Italy	Fr	(H)	2–0
1950	Scotland	HC/WCq	(A)	1–0
	Portugal	Fr	(A)	5–3
	Belgium	Fr	(A)	4–1
	Chile	WC	(N)	2–0
	USA	WC	(N)	0–1
	Spain	WC	(N)	0–1
	N Ireland	HC	(A)	4–1
	Wales	HC	(H)	4–2
	Yugoslavia	Fr	(H)	2–2
1951	Scotland	HC	(H)	2–3
	Argentina	Fr	(H)	2–1
	Portugal	Fr	(H)	5–2
	France	Fr	(H)	2–2
	Wales	HC	(A)	1–1
	N Ireland	HC	(H)	2–0
	Austria	Fr	(H)	2–2
1952	Scotland	HC	(A)	2–1
	Italy	Fr	(A)	1–1
	Austria	Fr	(A)	3–2
	Switzerland	Fr	(A)	3–0
	N Ireland	HC	(A)	2–2
	Wales	HC	(H)	5–2
	Belgium	Fr	(H)	5–0
1953	Scotland	HC	(H)	2–2
	Argentina	Fr	(A)	0–0 (Abandoned)
	Chile	Fr	(A)	2–1
	Uruguay	Fr	(A)	1–2
	USA	Fr	(A)	6–3
	Wales	HC/WCq	(A)	4–1
	Rest of Europe	Fr	(H)	4–4
	N Ireland	HC/WCq	(H)	3–1
	Hungary	Fr	(H)	3–6
1954	Scotland	HC/WCq	(A)	4–2
	Yugoslavia	Fr	(A)	0–1
	Hungary	Fr	(A)	1–7
	Belgium	WC	(N)	4–4*
	Switzerland	WC	(A)	2–0
	Uruguay	WC	(N)	2–4
	N Ireland	HC	(A)	2–0
	Wales	HC	(H)	3–2
	West Germany	Fr	(H)	3–1
1955	Scotland	HC	(H)	7–2
	France	Fr	(A)	0–1
	Spain	Fr	(A)	1–1
	Portugal	Fr	(A)	1–3
	Denmark	Fr	(A)	5–1
	Wales	HC	(A)	1–2
	N Ireland	HC	(H)	3–0
	Spain	Fr	(H)	4–1
1956	Scotland	HC	(A)	1–1
	Brazil	Fr	(H)	4–2
	Sweden	Fr	(A)	0–1

	Finland	Fr	(A)	5–1
	West Germany	Fr	(A)	3–1
	N Ireland	HC	(A)	1–1
	Wales	HC	(H)	3–1
	Yugoslavia	Fr	(H)	3–0
	Denmark	WCq	(H)	5–2
1957	Scotland	HC	(H)	2–1
	Republic Ireland	WCq	(H)	5–1
	Denmark	WCq	(A)	4–1
	Republic Ireland	WCq	(A)	1–1
	Wales	HC	(A)	4–0
	N Ireland	HC	(H)	2–3
	France	Fr	(H)	4–0
1958	Scotland	HC	(A)	4–0
	Portugal	Fr	(H)	2–1
	Yugoslavia	Fr	(A)	0–5
	USSR	Fr	(A)	1–1
	USSR	WC	(N)	2–2
	Brazil	WC	(N)	0–0
	Austria	WC	(N)	2–2
	USSR	WC	(N)	0–1
	N Ireland	HC	(A)	3–3
	USSR	Fr	(H)	5–0
	Wales	HC	(H)	2–2
1959	Scotland	HC	(H)	1–0
	Italy	Fr	(H)	2–2
	Brazil	Fr	(A)	0–2
	Peru	Fr	(A)	1–4
	Mexico	Fr	(A)	1–2
	USA	Fr	(A)	8–1
	Wales	HC	(A)	1–1
	Sweden	Fr	(H)	2–3
	N Ireland	HC	(H)	2–1
1960	Scotland	HC	(A)	1–1
	Yugoslavia	Fr	(H)	3–3
	Spain	Fr	(A)	0–3
	Hungary	Fr	(A)	0–2
	N Ireland	HC	(A)	5–2
	Luxembourg	WCq	(A)	9–0
	Spain	Fr	(H)	4–2
	Wales	HC	(H)	5–1
1961	Scotland	HC	(H)	9–3
	Mexico	Fr	(H)	8–0
	Portugal	WCq	(A)	1–1
	Italy	Fr	(A)	3–2
	Austria	Fr	(A)	1–3
	Luxembourg	WCq	(H)	4–1
	Wales	HC	(A)	1–1
	Portugal	WCq	(H)	2–0
	N Ireland	HC	(H)	1–1
1962	Austria	Fr	(H)	3–1
	Scotland	HC	(A)	0–2
	Switzerland	Fr	(H)	3–1

	Opponent	Type	Venue/Score
	Peru	Fr	(A) 4–0
	Hungary	WC	(N) 1–2
	Argentina	WC	(N) 3–1
	Bulgaria	WC	(N) 0–0
	Brazil	WC	(N) 1–3
	France	EC	(H) 1–1
	N Ireland	HC	(A) 3–1
	Wales	HC	(H) 4–0
1963	France	EC	(A) 2–5
	Scotland	HC	(H) 1–2
	Brazil	Fr	(H) 1–1
	Czechoslovakia	Fr	(A) 4–2
	East Germany	Fr	(A) 2–1
	Switzerland	Fr	(A) 8–1
	Wales	HC	(A) 4–0
	Rest of World	Fr	(H) 2–1
	N Ireland	HC	(H) 8–3
1964	Scotland	HC	(A) 0–1
	Uruguay	Fr	(H 2–1
	Portugal	Fr	(A) 4–3
	USA	Fr	(A) 10–0
	Brazil	T	(A) 1–5
	Portugal	T	(N) 1–1
	Argentina	T	(N) 0–1
	N Ireland	HC	(A) 4–3
	Belgium	Fr	(H) 2–2
	Wales	HC	(H) 2–1
	Holland	Fr	(A) 1–1
1965	Scotland	HC	(H) 2–2
	Hungary	Fr	(H) 1–0
	Yugoslavia	Fr	(A) 1–1
	West Germany	Fr	(A) 1–0
	Sweden	Fr	(A) 2–1
	Wales	HC	(A) 0–0
	Austria	Fr	(H) 2–3
	N Ireland	HC	(H) 2–1
	Spain	Fr	(A) 2–0
1966	Poland	Fr	(H) 1–1
	West Germany	Fr	(H) 1–0
	Scotland	HC	(A) 4–3
	Yugoslavia	Fr	(H) 2–0
	Finland	Fr	(A) 3–0
	Norway	Fr	(A) 6–1
	Denmark	Fr	(A) 2–0
	Poland	Fr	(A) 1–0
	Uruguay	WC	(H) 0–0
	Mexico	WC	(H) 2–0
	France	WC	(H) 2–0
	Argentina	WC	(H) 1–0
	Portugal	WC	(H) 2–1
	West Germany	WC	(H) 4–2*
	N Ireland	HC/ECq	(A) 2–0
	Czechoslovakia	Fr	(H) 0–0

	Wales	HC/ECq	(H) 5–1
1967	Scotland	HC/ECq	(H) 2–3
	Spain	Fr	(H) 2–0
	Austria	Fr	(A) 1–0
	Wales	HC/ECq	(A) 3–0
	N Ireland	HC/ECq	(H) 2–0
1968	USSR	Fr	(H) 2–2
	Scotland	HC/ECq	(A) 1–1
	Spain	EC	(H) 1–0
	Spain	EC	(A) 2–1
	Sweden	Fr	(H) 3–1
	West Germany	Fr	(A) 0–1
	Yugoslavia	EC	(N) 0–1
	USSR	EC	(N) 2–0
	Romania	Fr	(A) 0–0
	Bulgaria	Fr	(H) 1–1
1969	Romania	Fr	(H) 1–1
	France	Fr	(H) 5–0
	N Ireland	HC	(A) 3–1
	Wales	HC	(H) 2–1
	Scotland	HC	(H) 4–1
	Mexico	Fr	(A) 0–0
	Uruguay	Fr	(A) 2–1
	Brazil	Fr	(A) 1–2
	Holland	Fr	(A) 1–0
	Portugal	Fr	(H) 1–0
1970	Holland	Fr	(H) 0–0
	Belgium	Fr	(A) 3–1
	Wales	HC	(A) 1–1
	N Ireland	HC	(H) 3–1
	Scotland	HC	(A) 0–0
	Colombia	Fr	(A) 4–0
	Ecuador	Fr	(A) 2–0
	Romania	WC	(N) 1–0
	Brazil	WC	(N) 0–1
	Czechoslovakia	WC	(N) 1–0
	West Germany	WC	(N) 2–3*
	East Germany	Fr	(H) 3–1
1971	Malta	ECq	(A) 1–0
	Greece	ECq	(H) 3–0
	Malta	ECq	(H) 5–0
	N Ireland	HC	(A) 1–0
	Wales	HC	(H) 0–0
	Scotland	HC	(H) 3–1
	Switzerland	ECq	(A) 3–2
	Switzerland	ECq	(H) 1–1
	Greece	ECq	(A) 2–0
1972	West Germany	EC	(H) 1–3
	West Germany	EC	(A) 0–0
	Wales	HC	(A) 3–0
	N Ireland	HC	(H) 0–1
	Scotland	HC	(A) 1–0
	Yugoslavia	Fr	(H) 1–1

	Wales	WCq	(A) 1–0
1973	Wales	WCq	(H) 1–1
	Scotland	Fr	(A) 5–0
	N Ireland	HC	(H) 2–1
	Wales	HC	(H) 3–0
	Scotland	HC	(H) 1–0
	Czechoslovakia	Fr	(A) 1–1
	Poland	WCq	(A) 0–2
	USSR	Fr	(A) 2–1
	Italy	Fr	(A) 0–2
	Austria	Fr	(H) 7–0
	Poland	WCq	(H) 1–1
	Italy	Fr	(H) 0–1
1974	Portugal	Fr	(A) 0–0
	Wales	HC	(H) 2–0
	N Ireland	HC	(H) 1–0
	Scotland	HC	(A) 0–2
	Argentina	Fr	(H) 2–2
	East Germany	Fr	(A) 1–1
	Bulgaria	Fr	(A) 1–0
	Yugoslavia	Fr	(A) 2–2
	Czechoslovakia	ECq	(H) 3–0
	Portugal	ECq	(H) 0–0
1975	West Germany	Fr	(H) 2–0
	Cyprus	ECq	(H) 5–0
	Cyprus	ECq	(A) 1–0
	N Ireland	HC	(A) 0–0
	Wales	HC	(H) 2–2
	Scotland	HC	(H) 5–1
	Switzerland	Fr	(A) 2–1
	Czechoslovakia	ECq	(A) 1–2
	Portugal	ECq	(A) 1–1
1976	Wales	Fr	(A) 2–1
	Wales	HC	(A) 1–0
	N Ireland	HC	(H) 4–0
	Scotland	HC	(A) 1–2
	Brazil	T	(N) 0–1
	Italy	T	(N) 3–2
	Finland	WCq	(A) 4–1
	Republic Ireland	Fr	(H) 1–1
	Finland	WCq	(H) 2–1
	Italy	WCq	(A) 0–2
1977	Holland	Fr	(H) 0–2
	Luxembourg	WCq	(H) 5–0
	N Ireland	HC	(A) 2–1
	Wales	HC	(H) 0–1
	Scotland	HC	(H) 1–2
	Brazil	Fr	(A) 0–0
	Argentina	Fr	(A) 1–1
	Uruguay	Fr	(A) 0–0
	Switzerland	Fr	(A) 0–0
	Luxembourg	WCq	(A) 2–0
	Italy	WCq	(H) 2–0

1978	West Germany	Fr	(A)	1–2
	Brazil	Fr	(H)	1–1
	Wales	HC	(A)	3–1
	N Ireland	HC	(H)	1–0
	Scotland	HC	(A)	1–0
	Hungary	Fr	(H)	4–1
	Denmark	ECq	(A)	4–3
	Republic Ireland	ECq	(A)	1–1
	Czechoslovakia	Fr	(H)	1–0
1979	N Ireland	ECq	(H)	4–0
	N Ireland	HC	(A)	2–0
	Wales	HC	(H)	0–0
	Scotland	HC	(H)	3–1
	Bulgaria	ECq	(A)	3–0
	Sweden	Fr	(A)	0–0
	Austria	Fr	(A)	3–4
	Denmark	ECq	(H)	1–0
	N Ireland	ECq	(A)	5–1
	Bulgaria	ECq	(H)	2–0
1980	Republic Ireland	ECq	(H)	2–0
	Spain	Fr	(A)	2–0
	Argentina	Fr	(H)	3–1
	Wales	HC	(A)	1–4
	N Ireland	HC	(H)	1–1
	Scotland	HC	(A)	2–0
	Australia	Fr	(A)	2–1
	Belgium	EC	(N)	1–1
	Italy	EC	(A)	0–1
	Spain	EC	(N)	2–1
	Norway	WCq	(H)	4–0
	Romania	WCq	(A)	1–2
	Switzerland	WCq	(H)	2–1
1981	Spain	Fr	(H)	1–2
	Romania	WCq	(H)	0–0
	Brazil	Fr	(H)	0–1
	Wales	HC	(H)	0–0
	Scotland	HC	(H)	0–1
	Switzerland	WCq	(A)	1–2
	Hungary	WCq	(A)	3–1
	Norway	WCq	(A)	1–2
	Hungary	WCq	(H)	1–0
1982	N Ireland	HC	(H)	4–0
	Wales	HC	(A)	1–0
	Holland	Fr	(H)	2–0
	Scotland	HC	(A)	1–0
	Iceland	Fr	(A)	1–1
	Finland	Fr	(A)	4–1
	France	WC	(N)	3–1
	Czechoslovakia	WC	(N)	2–0
	Kuwait	WC	(N)	1–0
	West Germany	WC	(N)	0–0
	Spain	WC	(N)	0–0
	Denmark	ECq	(A)	2–2

	West Germany............Fr	(H) 1–2
	Greece ....ECq...........	(A) 3–0
	Luxembourg ....ECq...........	(H) 9–0
1983	Wales ....HC	(H) 2–1
	Greece ....ECq...........	(H) 0–0
	Hungary ....ECq...........	(H) 2–0
	N Ireland ....HC	(A) 0–0
	Scotland ....HC	(H) 2–0
	Australia....................Fr	(A) 0–0
	Australia....................Fr	(A) 1–0
	Australia....................Fr	(A) 1–1
	Denmark....................ECq...........	(H) 0–1
	Hungary ....ECq...........	(A) 3–0
	Luxembourg ....ECq...........	(A) 4–0
1984	France ....Fr	(A) 0–2
	N Ireland ....HC	(H) 1–0
	Wales ....HC	(A) 0–1
	Scotland ....HC	(A) 1–1
	USSR........................Fr	(H) 0–2
	Brazil........................Fr	(A) 2–0
	Uruguay ....Fr	(A) 0–2
	Chile ....Fr	(A) 0–0
	East Germany............Fr	(H) 1–0
	Finland......................WCq	(H) 5–0
	Turkey......................WCq	(A) 8–0
1985	N Ireland ....WCq	(A) 1–0
	Republic Ireland ....Fr	(H) 2–1
	Romania ....WCq	(A) 0–0
	Finland......................WCq	(A) 1–1
	Scotland....................RC............	(A) 0–1
	Italy........................T..............	(N) 1–2
	Mexico ....T..............	(A) 0–1
	West Germany............Fr	(N) 3–0
	USA..........................Fr	(A) 5–0
	Romania ....WCq	(H) 1–1
	Turkey......................WCq	(H) 5–0
	N Ireland ....WCq	(H) 0–0
1986	Egypt........................Fr	(A) 4–0
	Israel ....Fr	(A) 2–1
	USSR........................Fr	(A) 1–0
	Scotland....................RC............	(H) 2–1
	Mexico ....Fr	(N) 3–0
	Canada......................Fr	(A) 1–0
	Portugal ....WC	(N) 0–1
	Morocco ....WC	(N) 0–0
	Poland......................WC	(N) 3–0
	Paraguay ....WC	(N) 3–0
	Argentina ....WC	(N) 1–2
	Sweden ....Fr	(A) 0–1
	N Ireland ....ECq...........	(H) 3–0
	Yugoslavia ....ECq...........	(H) 2–0
1987	Spain ....Fr	(A) 4–2
	N Ireland ....ECq...........	(A) 2–0

	Opponent	Type	Venue	Score
	Turkey	ECq	(A)	0–0
	Brazil	RC	(H)	1–1
	Scotland	RC	(A)	0–0
	West Germany	Fr	(A)	1–3
	Turkey	ECq	(H)	8–0
	Yugoslavia	ECq	(A)	4–1
1988	Israel	Fr	(A)	0–0
	Holland	Fr	(H)	2–2
	Hungary	Fr	(A)	0–0
	Scotland	RC	(H)	1–0
	Colombia	RC	(H)	1–1
	Switzerland	Fr	(A)	1–0
	Republic Ireland	EC	(N)	0–1
	Holland	EC	(N)	1–3
	USSR	EC	(N)	1–3
	Denmark	Fr	(H)	1–0
	Sweden	WCq	(H)	0–0
	Saudi Arabia	Fr	(A)	1–1
1989	Greece	Fr	(A)	2–1
	Albania	WCq	(A)	2–0
	Albania	WCq	(H)	5–0
	Chile	RC	(H)	0–0
	Scotland	RC	(A)	2–0
	Poland	WCq	(H)	3–0
	Denmark	Fr	(A)	1–1
	Sweden	WCq	(A)	0–0
	Poland	WCq	(A)	0–0
	Italy	Fr	(H)	0–0
	Yugoslavia	Fr	(H)	2–1
1990	Brazil	Fr	(H)	1–0
	Czechoslovakia	Fr	(H)	4–2
	Denmark	Fr	(H)	1–0
	Uruguay	Fr	(H)	1–2
	Tunisia	Fr	(A)	1–1
	Republic Ireland	WC	(N)	1–1
	Holland	WC	(N)	0–0
	Egypt	WC	(N)	1–0
	Belgium	WC	(N)	1–0*
	Cameroon	WC	(N)	3–2*
	West Germany	WC	(N)	1–1*^
	Italy	WC	(N)	1–2
	Hungary	Fr	(H)	1–0
	Poland	ECq	(H)	2–0
	Republic Ireland	ECq	(A)	1–1
1991	Cameroon	Fr	(H)	2–0
	Republic Ireland	ECq	(H)	1–1
	Turkey	ECq	(A)	1–0
	USSR	T	(H)	3–1
	Argentina	T	(H)	2–2
	Australia	Fr	(A)	1–0
	New Zealand	Fr	(A)	1–0
	New Zealand	Fr	(A)	2–0
	Malaysia	Fr	(A)	4–2

	Germany	Fr	(H) 1–0
	Turkey	ECq	(H) 1–0
	Poland	ECq	(A) 1–1
1992	France	Fr	(H) 2–0
	Czechoslovakia	Fr	(A) 2–2
	CIS	Fr	(A) 2–2
	Hungary	Fr	(A) 1–0
	Brazil	Fr	(H) 1–1
	Finland	Fr	(A) 2–1
	Denmark	EC	(N) 0–0
	France	EC	(N) 0–0
	Sweden	EC	(A) 1–2
	Spain	Fr	(A) 0–1
	Norway	WCq	(H) 1–1
	Turkey	WCq	(H) 4–0
1993	San Marino	WCq	(H) 6–0
	Turkey	WCq	(A) 2–0
	Holland	WCq	(H) 2–2
	Poland	WCq	(A) 1–1
	Norway	WCq	(A) 0–2
	USA	T	(A) 0–2
	Brazil	T	(N) 1–1
	Germany	T	(N) 1–2
	Poland	WCq	(H) 3–0
	Holland	WCq	(A) 0–2
	San Marino	WCq	(A) 7–1
1994	Demark	Fr	(H) 1–0
	Greece	Fr	(H) 5–0
	Norway	Fr	(H) 0–0
	USA	Fr	(H) 2–0
	Romania	Fr	(H) 1–1
	Nigeria	Fr	(H) 1–0
1995	Republic Ireland	Fr	(A) 0–1 (Abandoned)
	Uruguay	Fr	(H) 0–0
	Japan	T	(H) 2–1
	Sweden	T	(H) 3–3
	Brazil	T	(H) 1–3
	Colombia	Fr	(H) 0–0
	Norway	Fr	(A) 0–0
	Switzerland	Fr	(H) 3–1
	Portugal	Fr	(H) 1–1
1996	Bulgaria	Fr	(H) 1–0
	Croatia	Fr	(H) 0–0
	Hungary	Fr	(H) 3–0
	China	Fr	(A) 3–0
	Switzerland	EC	(H) 1–1
	Scotland	EC	(H) 2–0
	Holland	EC	(H) 4–1
	Spain	EC	(H) 0–0*+
	Germany	EC	(H) 1–1*^
	Moldova	WCq	(A) 3–0
	Poland	WCq	(H) 2–1
	Georgia	WCq	(A) 2–0

1997	Italy	WCq	(H) 0–1
	Mexico	Fr	(H) 2–0
	Georgia	WCq	(H) 2–0
	South Africa	Fr	(H) 2–1
	Poland	WCq	(A) 2–0
	Italy	T	(N) 2–0
	France	T	(A) 1–0
	Brazil	T	(N) 0–1
	Moldova	WCq	(H) 4–0
	Italy	WCq	(A) 0–0
1998	Chile	Fr	(H) 0–2
	Switzerland	Fr	(A) 1–1
	Portugal	Fr	(H) 3–0
	Saudi Arabia	Fr	(H) 0–0
	Morocco	T	(A) 1–0
	Belgium	T	(N) 0–0^
	Tunisia	WC	(N) 2–0
	Romania	WC	(N) 1–2
	Colombia	WC	(N) 2–0
	Argentina	WC	(N) 2–2*^
	Sweden	ECq	(A) 1–2
	Bulgaria	ECq	(H) 0–0
	Luxembourg	ECq	(A) 3–0
1999	France	Fr	(H) 0–2
	Poland	ECq	(H) 3–1
	Hungary	Fr	(A) 1–1
	Sweden	ECq	(H) 0–0
	Bulgaria	ECq	(A) 1–1
	Luxembourg	ECq	(H) 6–0
	Poland	ECq	(A) 0–0
	Belgium	ECq	(H) 2–1
	Scotland	ECq	(A) 2–0
	Scotland	ECq	(H) 0–1
2000	Argentina	Fr	(H) 0–0
	Brazil	Fr	(H) 1–1
	Ukraine	Fr	(H) 2–0
	Malta	Fr	(A) 2–1
	Portugal	EC	(N) 2–3
	Germany	EC	(N) 1–0
	Romania	EC	(N) 2–3
	France	Fr	(A) 1–1
	Germany	WCq	(H) 0–1
	Finland	WCq	(A) 0–0
	Italy	Fr	(A) 0–1
2001	Spain	Fr	(H) 3–0
	Finland	WCq	(H) 2–1
	Albania	WCq	(A) 3–1
	Mexico	Fr	(H) 4–0
	Greece	WCq	(A) 2–0
	Holland	Fr	(H) 0–2
	Germany	WCq	(A) 5–1
	Albania	WCq	(H) 2–0
	Greece	WCq	(H) 2–2

	Sweden .... Fr .... (H) 1–1
2002	Holland .... Fr .... (A) 1–1
	Italy .... Fr .... (H) 1–2
	Paraguay .... Fr .... (H) 4–0
	South Korea .... Fr .... (A) 1–1
	Cameroon .... Fr .... (N) 2–2
	Sweden .... WC .... (N) 1–1
	Argentina .... WC .... (N) 1–0
	Nigeria .... WC .... (N) 0–0
	Denmark .... WC .... (N) 3–0
	Brazil .... WC .... (N) 1–2
	Portugal .... Fr .... (H) 1–1
	Slovakia .... ECq .... (A) 2–1
	Macedonia .... ECq .... (H) 2–2
2003	Liechenstein .... ECq .... (A) 2–0
	Turkey .... ECq .... (H) 2–0
	South Africa .... Fr .... (A) 2–1
	Serbia & .... Fr .... (H) 2–1
	Montenegro ....
	Slovakia .... ECq .... (H) 2–1
	Croatia .... Fr .... (H) 3–1
	Macedonia .... ECq .... (A) 2–1
	Liechenstein .... ECq .... (H) 2–0
	Turkey .... ECq .... (A) 0–0
	Denmark .... Fr .... (H) 2–3
2004	Portugal .... Fr .... (A) 1–1
	Sweden .... Fr .... (A) 0–1
	Japan .... Fr .... (H) 1–1
	Iceland .... Fr .... (H) 6–1
	France .... EC .... (N) 1–2
	Switzerland .... EC .... (N) 3–0
	Croatia .... EC .... (N) 4–2
	Portugal .... EC .... (A) 2–2*^
	Ukraine .... Fr .... (H) 3–0
	Austria .... WCq .... (A) 2–2
	Poland .... WCq .... (A) 2–1
	Wales .... WCq .... (H) 2–0
	Azerbaijan .... WCq .... (A) 1–0
	Spain .... Fr .... (A) 0–1
2005	Holland .... Fr .... (H) 0–0
	N Ireland .... WCq .... (H) 4–0
	Azerbaijan .... WCq .... (H) 2–0
	USA .... Fr .... (A) 2–1
	Colombia .... Fr .... (N) 3–2
	Denmark .... Fr .... (A) 1–4
	Wales .... WCq .... (A) 1–0
	N Ireland .... WCq .... (A) 0–1
	Austria .... WCq .... (H) 1–0
	Poland .... WCq .... (H) 2–1
	Argentina .... Fr .... (N) 3–2

— SELECTED BIBLIOGRAPHY —

Adams, Tony, *Addicted* (HarperCollins, 1998)

Allen, Peter, *An Amber Glow: The Story of England's World Cup-winning Football* (Mainstream Publishing, 2000)

Armfield, Jimmy, *Right Back to the Beginning* (Headline Book Publishing, 2004)

Ball, Alan, *Playing Extra Time* (Sidgwick & Jackson Ltd, 2004)

Banks, Gordon, *Banks: The Autobiography* (Michael Joseph, 2002)

Butcher, Terry, *Butcher: My Autobiography* (Highdown, 2005)

Cohen, George, *My Autobiography* (Greenwater Publising Ltd, 2003)

Davies, Pete, *All Played Out: The Full Story of Italia '90* (William Heinemann Ltd, 1990)

Drewett, Jim and Leith, Alex, *The Book of Virgin Football Records* (Virgin Books, 1996)

Edworthy, Niall, *The Second Most Important Job in the Country* (Virgin Publishing Ltd, 1999)

Edworthy, Niall, *England, The Official FA History* (Virgin Books, 1997)

Finney, Tom, *Autobiography* (Headline Book Publishing, 2003)

Football Association, *The Complete Guide to England Players since 1945* (Stanley Paul, 1993)

Gascoigne, Paul, *Gazza: My Story* (Headline Book Publishing, 2004)

Giller, Norman, *Billy Wright: A Hero for All Seasons* (Robson Books, 2002)

Giller, Norman, *Football and All That* (Hodder & Stoughton Ltd, 2004)

Glanville, Brian, *The Story of the World Cup* (Faber and Faber Limited, 1997)

Greaves, Jimmy, *Greavsie, The Autobiography* (Time Warner Books, 2003)

Heatley, Michael and Welch, Ian, *England Football* (Dial House, 1996)

Hoddle, Glenn and Davies, David, *My 1998 World Cup Diary* (Andre Deutsch Ltd, 1998)

Hurst, Geoff, *1966 and All That* (Headline Book Publishing, 2001)

Keegan, Kevin, *My Autobiography* (Little, Brown & Co. 1997)

Leatherdale, Clive, *England, The Quest for the World Cup* (Two Heads Publishing, 1994)

MacDonald, Malcolm, *Supermac* (Highdown, 2003)

Matthews, Stanley, *The Way It Was: My Autobiography* (Headline Book Publishing, 2000)

Pearce, Stuart, *Psycho* (Headline Book Publishing, 2000)

Pickering, David, *The Cassell Soccer Companion* (Cassell, 1994)

Robson, Bobby, *Farewell But Not Goodbye* (Hodder & Stoughton, 2005)

Shaw, Phil, *The Book of Football Quotations* (Ebury Press, 2003)

Shearer, Alan, *My Story So Far* (Hodder and Stoughton, 1998)

Shilton, Peter, *My Autobiography* (Orion, 2004)

Signy, Dennis, *A Pictorial History of Soccer* (Hamlyn Publishing Group Limited, 1968)

Stiles, Nobby, *After the Ball: My Autobiography* (Sceptre, 2003)

Watt, Tom and Palmer, Kevin *Wembley: The Greatest Stage* (Simon & Schuster, 1998)

Woolnough, Brian, *The Inside Story of Kevin Keegan and England* (Ebury Press, 2000)